JUDY'S WORLD

JUDY'S WORLD

The World of Autism
Through the Eyes of a Mother

JUDY BLAKE

JUDY BLAKE
www.judysworld.info

Manufactured in the United States of America

10 9 8 7 6 5 4 3 2 1

Edited by Victoria Miller
Cover Design & Layout by Anthony Sclavi
www.briobooks.com

International Standard Book Number
ISBN 13: 978-0-615-49711-2

Dedication

Judy's World is dedicated to my two amazing kids, Jason and Ryan. They are so special and I could not imagine life without them. They have a loving father who has helped them be the wonderful sons they are today. We are blessed to have loving grandparents, extended family, and friends. Their support through the years has meant the world to us.

It takes a village to raise all children and this book is dedicated to everyone who has helped our family. Without the initial diagnosis and guidance of Dr. Danny Williamson, we would not have been able to get our kids the help that they needed. The countless teachers, speech therapists, occupational therapists, diagnosticians—each one of them made a difference in the lives of my kids.

In loving memory of Jane Stewart, one of the most devoted advocates of special needs children and their families. Founder of the Westview School, she helped my family in the early years and we will never forget her love and passion for all of her students.

To Deborah Bahme, thank you for the countless hours you spent helping me work through my thoughts and ideas to finish this book.

To Deborah Horwitz, thank you for your creativity and inspiration in helping me design the book cover.

To my amazing mother, you are the best mother that any daughter could ever hope for.

To my boyfriend, Craig, who is the love of my life—you inspire me every day and I thank G-d that you are in our lives.

Contents

Introduction

Why I Wanted to Share my Story

My family and friends have told me for years that I needed to write this book and share with others what my kids experience, and how I help them through each day. I've always been a very realistic person and I call it like I see it—it is what it is. While I knew I had to accept my life as it was, there were so many days when I truly wondered if I was going to make it. Yes, I am a strong person, but everyone has their limits. Through it all, one of the most important things I always tried to do was remain calm. Trust me; this was not an easy feat. It's very easy to yell when you're at the end of your rope and frustrated beyond belief. I'd be lying if I told you I didn't have some of those days and felt absolutely awful for acting that way. I knew that I was only human, but I didn't want to be at times like this. I wanted to have the patience of Job at all times.

Some of the stories you are about to read you won't believe, some you will laugh at, and some will make you sad. This doesn't surprise me. I've always said that if I ever wrote a book, everyone would think it was fiction. But these stories are true, every single one. There is no way I could create these even in my wildest dreams. Some stories will make you laugh, and that's okay. Some people get embarrassed when I tell them stories and they start to giggle. They're afraid that I'll feel they're being insensitive. Nothing could be further from the truth. I laugh at what goes on in my life. Laughter is a good thing. And if I don't laugh, I'll cry. Laughing at something doesn't always mean you're showing disrespect or being unkind. Some of the statements my kids have made or things they have done truly are too funny. My laughter is not an attempt to make fun of them. It is simply my way of coping with what has transpired. We all know that kids can say and do the darnedest things.

The mission of this book is to raise awareness of and compassion for those coping with special needs that cannot be seen. As a society, we tend to be more compassionate toward someone who uses a cane, is in a wheelchair, or has a cast or brace. Their difficulties are visible and therefore exist tangibly, so there is less of a rush to judgment. But what about the struggles people encounter that can't be seen? One goal of this book is to break the stereotypes people hold when they "think" they know about those with special needs.

As you join me on my journey, please do not feel sorry for me. I'm not writing this book because I want you to pity my children or me. My children are precious and I could not imagine my life without them. They are bright and have so much to offer this world. I want to open your eyes, open your mind, and most of all, open your heart.

Welcome to my world!

The mission of this book is to raise awareness of and compassion for those coping with special needs that cannot be seen. As a society, we tend to be more compassionate toward someone who uses a cane, is in a wheelchair, or has a cast or brace. Their difficulties are visible, and therefore exist tangibly so there is less of a rush to judgment. But what about the struggles people encounter that can't be seen?

I am the single parent of two boys with special needs, ages 19 and 16. I am not a doctor, nor a speech therapist, or a psychologist. I haven't conducted any long-term studies or published any papers in the Journal of American Medicine. I'm just a mom and have two boys diagnosed with autism. In addition, they also cope with impulsiveness, anxiety and Obsessive-Compulsive Disorder (OCD). It's not uncommon for kids on the autism spectrum to battle a multitude of issues in conjunction with their autism. For my older son, he also struggles with Attention Deficit Hyperactivity Disorder (ADHD) which complicates matters even more for him.

Who hasn't been at a restaurant or shopping mall and believed a misbehaving child was out of control? Who hasn't thought that the child was too old to be throwing temper tantrums or wondered why the parent wasn't doing more? The child looks perfectly normal. There is nothing the eye can see to infer that the child had any medical issues. It seems the child is acting spoiled. Since it appears that there's nothing wrong with the child, it must be the parents did not know how to take care of their child or indeed, the child is acting like a brat for no reason at all.

This is where the problem begins! People automatically assume that they know what is going on. But we must remember that we don't know the whole story. One goal of this book is to break the stereotypes people hold when they "think" they know about those with special needs. Typically, we only regard only the physical problems of those around us. If someone with Down's syndrome or cerebral palsy is having difficulties, we tend to understand them more readily. Their behavior is justified in our minds because we can see that they have special needs. It is human nature to be sensitive when someone is physically different.

For those who have hidden disabilities, it is more complicated. The expression "You don't know what goes on behind closed doors" can be modified to describe a person coping with special needs. "You don't know what is going on inside that person" – everything is not always as it appears to be. So where does this leave us? I'm not asking for people to make excuses for those who act inappropriately; we all know people who can be demanding and impossible because they want something done their way or believe they are always right.

So how do you know if the person acting inappropriately has special needs? It's not always easy to tell – but most people assume they will just know. They know why a child is acting unruly and are the self-proclaimed expert. Some believe they would automatically know if a child has special needs. This is not the case as I have been wrongly judged with my own children and other parents in my shoes have experienced the same problem.

In order to combat this rush to judgment, it's important to define the following concepts. Compassion - deep awareness of the suffering of another. Understanding - disposition to appreciate or share the feelings and thoughts of others. In my efforts to educate those around me, I will always try to increase their compassion for and understanding of people different from them. When my kids were born, I think my natural empathy began to increase rapidly. We all think we would handle something differently if we were in another person's shoes. We know how we would react and how we would fix the problem. Then, our world changes and we're faced with something that we never saw coming. We try to keep our composure and act gracefully, but we're human and the pressure is enormous. In my case, I'm very grateful that my compassion and understanding has not been compromised. Sure, I have my days and even my weeks when I know I'm being tested way too much. It is very difficult to have patience at these very stressful times. But overall, I continue to have empathy and this has not wavered through the years. I come from a family that is loving and nurturing and believe this shaped the person that I am today.

If you are a parent, a grandparent, or even a friend of someone who has been recently diagnosed with a "hidden" disability, it is my hope that this book provides you with insight into what their world might be like. I would never assume that what my children have experienced is what other children will encounter. Nor do I assume that other parents will have the same thoughts and beliefs as I have. But what I have found is that there are a lot of similarities and in some cases, the stories we share are the same. There exists a special and unique bond between parents of special needs kids. You could meet another parent for the first time and it's clear there is just an understanding that is automatic, a connection that is immediately present. Connections like these are very comforting. You don't have to explain, don't have to justify, and you certainly don't have to worry what the other parent is thinking. They are living your life and understand where you are coming from.

Some of the stories you are about to read you won't believe, some you will laugh at, and some will make you sad. This doesn't surprise me. I've always said that if I ever wrote a book, everyone would think it was fiction. But these stories are true, every single one. There is no way I could create these even in my wildest dreams. The stories that will make you laugh, that's okay. Some people are embarrassed when I tell them stories and they start to giggle. They're afraid that I'll feel they're being insensitive. Nothing could be further from the truth. I laugh at what goes on in my life. Laughter is a good thing. And if I don't laugh, I'll cry. Laughing at something doesn't always mean you're showing disrespect or being unkind. Some of the statements my kids have made or things they have done truly are too funny. My laughing is not an attempt to make fun of them. It is simply my way of coping with what has transpired. We know that kids can say and do the darnedest things.

For the stories that will make you sad – they are heartbreaking. They're devastating for me and might be for you as well. The reality is that this is my life and my kids' too. As children, we all had moments that we wanted to forget and wish had never happened. As children get older, the problems grow bigger and they become even more complex. For typically developing kids, it is difficult at best. When your children have the odds stacked against them, it is challenging beyond belief.

Like with any story, you have to start at the beginning. And while I didn't receive the first diagnosis until my first son was 4 and a half years old, there is so much to tell you leading up to this time. There were so many moments of confusion and wondering why my child was behaving the way that he was. I've read several self-help and motivational books throughout the years; each one has inspired me and I've learned from others' experiences. I've read books on coping with death, children and divorce, raising children with autism and books on interpersonal relationships. In my ever so humble efforts to share my story, I hope I have been successful in writing a book that is easy for you to read, and one that you will learn from and enjoy. You will see that I am not a professional writer. I speak what is on my mind and what is in my heart. I write in laymen's terms and want to connect with as many readers as possible.

As you join me on my journey, please do not feel sorry for me. I'm not writing this book because I want you to pity my children or me. This is not my intention and certainly not my style. The goal is to educate and while I am not a teacher by degree, I try to teach people at every available opportunity.

My children are precious and I could not imagine my life without them. They are bright and have so much to offer this world. As any child grows into an adult, they can contribute to society. They may not grow at the same rate or in the same way, but we must not forget that every child is special and deserves a chance. My grandmother used to say to me, "No child ever asked to be brought into this world." And she was right!

Welcome to my world! Through the years, I've had to confront the same emotions as many of you. We've all had sadness, confusion, and stress. This is all part of life and mine is no different than yours. While I try very hard to be optimistic and see my glass as half full, I'd be lying if I told you I always felt this way. I have my moments of pain, anger, and disbelief. I imagine that we all feel this way at various times in our lives. But through it all, I try my very best to remember the positive, the happiness, and the love I have for my children, family, and friends.

I want to open your eyes, open your mind, and most of all, open your heart.

Enjoy the ride!

The First Few Years

I always believed that if a child was born with ten fingers and ten toes, you were in the clear. I was 29 years old when my first son was born on October 17, 1991. He was adorable and so tiny; he weighed only 5 lbs, 5 ounces. I used to call him a paperweight. Jason was the light of my life and being a mother was everything to me. We were living in Detroit and I was fortunate to be able to stay home with him and never took this for granted. Being a new parent is overwhelming and while it is a joyous time in life, it can be very scary. Even if you've taken care of children before, it's different this time. It is your child and solely your responsibility. People used to tell me that for being a first time mother, I was laid back. Don't get me wrong, I believed in structure. I had my rules and Jason was on a schedule. These things were important to me. I just wasn't the nervous type or one to worry at every moment over minor issues.

I took Jason everywhere with me: restaurants, shopping malls, and errands galore. I had friends who did not take their infants out nearly as much as I did; they feared they would get sick. I guess I didn't think about things like that. I went about my life and didn't wait for the other shoe to fall.

I just enjoyed being a mom and watching him grow. I can remember putting him on the floor and just watching him smile or play with a toy. I could watch him for hours and nothing else would get done. It was such an innocent time and life was so carefree. I think that's how it should be when a child is born. If they're healthy, just enjoy the moment. I was involved in a playgroup and loved getting together with the other moms and their babies. Most of us were first timers so our lives revolved around feeding schedules, diaper changes, and naps. I took Jason to Gymboree classes and loved doing that as well. Everything was great and I treasured this time in my life.

Like any responsible parent, I took my son for all of the regular checkups to make sure he was on track and I wasn't missing anything. He received the recommended immunizations and I followed the pediatrician's guidelines for diet and feeding times. I remember when the other babies in our playgroup began to reach for toys, sit up, and crawl. Of course I wondered why my child wasn't doing these things. I asked the doctor and was told that every child develops differently and at their own pace. There are ranges when babies and toddlers hit those milestones and those ranges exist for a reason.

It was no different when I was pregnant with Jason. I had morning sickness for the first 4 months. Some of my friends had it for 8 weeks and others didn't experience any. I gained 33 pounds during my pregnancy. I had friends who gained 23 pounds and others who gained 43. I remember reading a couple of great books during my pregnancy and the first year of motherhood. The books were "What to Expect When You're Expecting" and "What to Expect Your First Year". They were wonderful books and since it was my first pregnancy, I truly didn't know what to expect. Everyone is different during their pregnancy and it helped to read about what might happen during this time. Guidelines on what to expect the first year were fantastic and easy to follow. I learned that children develop at their own rate and in their own time. So I didn't think much of the delays during the first 6-8 months of his life.

I went about my life and activities, enjoying my child's first year with much happiness. We played with all of the latest and greatest toys that were brightly colored and educational. We had textured toys, toys that made noises, and toys with appropriate pictures. I believe I did all of the right things to promote his development. I read to him all of the time; our apartment was a hybrid of Toys"R"Us and a children's bookstore. One of the first milestones he hit was on March 3, 1992. He rolled over from his stomach to his back. We were elated! He was just shy of 5 months and I thought Jason was progressing well. When he turned 9 months old, he sat up! We were so excited, I remember calling friends and family and sharing the wonderful news.

I knew that by this time, other babies were already crawling and some were cruising while holding onto furniture. We weren't there yet but he was sitting up and I was happy to have reached that milestone. While he started to crawl backwards in August 1992, he didn't crawl well until November of that year. By this time, he was 13 months old and most of the other kids were either walking with assistance or even on their own. Our play group was a mixture of boys and girls and as you would expect, most of the girls were ahead of the boys. While I wondered when he would walk, all of the books and articles I read continued to tell me that all children develop at different times and in different ways. In June of 1993, we relocated to Northern Illinois for work-related reasons. By this time, Jason was 20 months old. He had just begun walking and we were thrilled.

I remember going for our last checkup before we moved and the pediatrician expressed concerns. He believed there were developmental issues but was not sure what the problem was. While it was wonderful that he was finally walking, he explained that Jason had moved beyond the normal range for achieving the initial milestones and felt we should seek additional help. My heart sank and I remember tears filled up my eyes. A doctor never wants to convey upsetting news to a parent but I'm very glad he did. I wanted to know his thoughts and appreciated his guidance. He was a wonderful doctor during this time in our lives and I truly respected his opinion.

I have never been the kind of mom who has her head in the sand. If you tell me something isn't right, I am the first to seek out help and resolve it as quickly as possible. I do know there are other parents who seem to postpone what they need to do or block out and hear what they want to hear. I couldn't do that and while I don't blame parents who do – this isn't making the problem go away. It is only delaying the inevitable. It is hard when it is your child; I've just always believed in confronting the issues head on. If the doctor told you your child had a vitamin deficiency or needed medicine for something, you would certainly address it. But when there is something developmental or emotional that is the issue, it can be difficult to take that next step to seek help. But not me. I was all over it.

As soon as we moved and were settled in, I connected with our new pediatrician and made sure she was well aware of our previous doctor's concerns. I also enrolled Jason in a wonderful preschool program that came highly recommended. I wanted him to socialize with his peers and learn from others. He attended three days a week and enjoyed it very much. His teachers were attentive and worked very hard to promote his development. But they were concerned about his development as well. In talking to them and to the pediatrician, it was recommended that I have him tested through our school district. I completed all of the necessary forms and had his preschool teachers do the same. It was important to have as much input as possible so that the diagnosticians testing him had a complete picture.

After administering several tests, I was told that he had delayed speech and a six-month delay in fine motor skills. The fine motor delay was not unusual for boys and I was told to keep an eye on it. They recommended that he receive speech therapy and I jumped on it. Within a few weeks, he was working with a speech therapist two days a week. I felt this helped and I worked with him at home as well. The speech therapist suggested ways to advance his speech so I could help him progress even more and I made sure we followed her home plan. He continued to receive speech therapy for about a year and his speech improved greatly.

Being in a new city, it was a blessing I was the outgoing type. Within a few months, Jason was already involved in a playgroup and also involved with some of the neighborhood kids as well. I made sure to have parents and their kids over so he was exposed as often as possible to his peers. We continued to have the "in" toys for boys his age and we read books a lot. I would read to him for hours at a time; he just loved it and couldn't get enough. I thought this was great. Reading opens up a child's mind in so many ways. So to me, the more you read to your child, the better. It got to the point that he could recite the pages himself from the pictures and if I misspoke, he immediately corrected me. I remember thinking to myself how wonderful it was that he was retaining the story line and truly engaged with it. Yes, at times, I felt it was a bit much that I would read the same seven books for hours at a time. But I was excited that he was fascinated and thought this was still okay.

Jason became interested in the most unusual things and his temperament became more intense. Between the ages of 3-4 years old, he became much more rigid. If our schedule changed, he became upset. If his favorite show was on at a different day or time, he became unglued. When he was upset, it was difficult to understand what he was trying to tell me. The teachers said he was a joy to have at school, which was a relief. But they, too, noticed that he would speak several random words at a time that made no sense or had nothing to do with the conversation at hand. He would just blurt out whatever was on his mind in no particular order. He had no clue what he was even saying sometimes and if people around him started to laugh, he had no idea why.

What I really began to notice was his obsession or attraction to unusual television shows. I've enjoyed watching the political shows on cable for many years. Back then, I used to watch "Equal Time," a Democrat vs. Republican debate of current issues and events. Jason actually loved listening to the opening music for the show and watching it with me. What 3 ½ year old child watches shows like this? I thought it was bizarre but didn't know what to think of it.

He did watch his share of Nickelodeon shows and plenty of Sesame Street and Barney tapes. These were all age appropriate so I truly believed in my mind that it all balanced out. I then realized that the Nickelodeon shows had become an obsession. We had to be home at a certain time to watch them. If we didn't, it was as though the world was coming to an end. I would set the VCR so that we weren't beholden to the television. I certainly didn't want our lives to revolve around that. This helped tremendously because if I forgot to record the show or set it for the wrong time, I could just pop in the old tape and he was happy. A catastrophe did occur when a show went off the air. You have no idea how devastating it was when he would turn on the channel at the correct time and a different show appeared. He became pretty hysterical! You would have thought he was bleeding or had a broken arm. He would scream and cry and was essentially inconsolable.

I didn't know what to do. I tried to explain to him that sometimes schedules change but that made no sense to him. Why would someone want to change a schedule? Why would you want something to be different than before? Don't you want to watch the same show at the same time all of the time? I realized this had become his world but I had no explanation as to why. It was a very confusing time and I didn't know of anyone else's child acting like this. Sure, all kids have temper tantrums and a routine is healthy. As I've said before, I believe in structure for children and practiced what I preached. Kids need to know their boundaries and what to expect. But none of the other kids were as obsessed or extreme as Jason.

I was perplexed every day and my days became very unpredictable. I never knew what would set him off and this was painful for me. As a mom, it was important that I understand my child, and help him learn and grow from his experiences. The teachers began to have some difficulty with him but he was still a very sweet child and this made all the difference in the world. They would correct him as needed and work with him to better interact with the other children. I continued with our regular visits to the pediatrician and discussed Jason's behavior with her. I also asked the speech therapist but no one seemed to know why Jason acted this way and believed it was just a phase.

I'm a huge believer in babysitters. I believe it's important for parents to have alone time without their children around. Yes, children are paramount in parents' lives but a marriage is, too. I bring this up because as much as I wanted to help Jason and as difficult as it was raising him during this time, I knew that I needed a break from him on the weekends. During the week, he was at his preschool program for three days. But the weekends were very long and I knew it was healthy for me to have some relief time. I'm fortunate that he did well with babysitters. He would watch his television shows, have stories read to him and they would put him to bed. Had there been difficulty with sitters, this would have been a problem. I was also fortunate that we had a great neighbor whose house he was very comfortable with. They were so understanding of Jason's peculiarities and took his quirky behavior in stride. I was grateful to them for all they did for us; they were our dear friends and very accepting of our family.

I became pregnant with our second child in the summer of 1994. I was so excited and so grateful that it was very easy for me to get pregnant. The downside, though, was that my morning sickness became all day sickness – not a fun time when I was also taking care of another child who deserved my time and attention. The constant nausea was a dominant force to be reckoned with. In the big picture, this was manageable and I wasn't complaining. I had friends who had struggled for years to have a child. My heart went out to them because I knew they tried so hard. It was painful to see them go through such a distressing time when their numerous attempts to have a child had failed.

In order to give Jason more of a life while I was feeling so sick, I increased his enrollment in preschool to five days a week. I wanted him engaged with others rather than sitting in front of the television while I was lying in bed or sick in the bathroom. I continued all of our other activities and knew how important the routine was to his well being. Overall, the pregnancy went well and the morning sickness subsided after a few months. I was back to my usual self and preparing Jason for his new sibling.

I think it's hard for any child to understand what it means when there is a baby inside of a mother's stomach. At times, Jason would grasp the concept and at times there was a disconnection. He continued to be rigid in his thinking and routine; I coped and managed as best I could. I made sure to review with him many times our plan for when I had to go to the hospital. He knew that he would go to our friend's house. She was wonderful with him and would make sure he had the foods he liked and his own television to watch his shows. I felt he was prepared and when the time came, there was no confusion and no outburst. Having Jason know what to expect made all the difference.

Then the time came; it was March 26, 1995. My water broke at home but it was happening at a very slow pace. We took Jason to our friend's house as planned. When we arrived at the hospital, I was examined by my doctor. He broke my water completely to move the labor process along. It didn't help much and he administered Pitocin. He was about to leave and check on another patient when he asked me if I felt the baby move. At that moment, I really didn't know. I didn't think I felt anything moving but wasn't sure. He immediately performed an internal ultrasound and realized I had a prolapsed cord. The baby went into distress and he performed an emergency C-section. Within minutes, Ryan was born. He appeared to be healthy and I was so grateful to my doctor for how he handled such a serious situation. It could have been much worse.

Within a few weeks before Ryan's birth, we found out we were relocating again and moving from Illinois to Houston. I was very concerned about how Jason would handle another major change. First, a new baby brother and now we were moving again. The first time we moved, he was only 18 months old so it was easier to manage. Now, it was a new home, new school, new city, new everything. I planned as much as I could to prepare him. We talked about it constantly and made sure to speak only positively about our move.

Overall, he did very well. I think that it helped reassuring him that all of his stuffed animals and toys would move right with him. He would be able to watch the same television shows and while they would be on a different numbered channel – Nickelodeon would be waiting for him at his new home. I also made sure that he and I spent time alone together those initial weeks after Ryan was born. Like any parent, you want to make sure your first child doesn't feel left out or neglected. I would buy him special presents and always remind him how much I loved him.

We moved in July of 1995 to Houston and life was very hectic. When I look back, it was certainly a very stressful time: recovering from a C-section, a newborn, an older child with an unpredictable personality, and moving to a new city.

But we all survived and settled into our home. I found a wonderful preschool and we joined our local Temple. It was great because we met other families with young children and this helped us to acclimate quickly. Jason started his new nursery school in mid-August. It was a fantastic school with a great reputation. It was part of our Temple, which was a huge plus. His teachers were enthusiastic, warm, and nurturing. I remember being so happy that I found this school for him.

At the same time, I wanted Ryan to have the same opportunities that Jason had. Within a few months, we were already involved in a play-group. I wanted to meet mothers that had newborns so Ryan could have future playmates. It didn't take long before I was involved in other activities with both kids, fully immersing myself in the community. Between "Mommy and Me" classes with Ryan, gymnastics classes for Jason, and family events at our Temple, our life was active and fulfilling.

Like most schools, they scheduled parent/teacher conferences about 8-10 weeks into the school year. I will never forget walking into the room and there sat Jason's two teachers, the preschool principal, and the headmaster of the entire school. With my quick humor, I told them that that I was honored to have so many teachers and administrators attend my son's first conference. Either they were going to tell me I had a child genius or that something was wrong.

As you would expect, it was the latter. They were very concerned that something wasn't right with Jason. They were very kind and gentle in how they told me. I reassured them that I was not surprised. They experienced some of the same problems I did. Jason had a lack of eye contact and seemed to be in another world sometimes. He had trouble communicating with the other children and with the teachers.

They all emphasized he was not a behavior problem and a very sweet child. In trying to teach him, they felt disconnected and he would begin talking about something that had nothing to do with the topic at hand. In their efforts to redirect him, he was still lost and could not be reached. They wondered what they were doing wrong because they were experienced teachers and their methods had worked for years with other students. Again, no one could tell me what the problem was; only that a problem existed and he needed help. While it was very hard for me to hear that his progress was in a holding pattern, I wanted them to be honest. This was my child and nothing was more important to me. It would be a disservice to him if I didn't get him the proper help. At the same time, I also didn't want to be unfair to his classmates.

The principal knew of a doctor who conducted developmental tests on children. While he was a pediatrician by degree, he didn't see children for colds, checkups, or immunizations. His specialty was the development of children and in addition to his medical degree, he had received additional training on social and milestone development. I remember being filled with so many emotions. I was relieved that someone might be able to tell me why Jason was the way he was yet nervous about what I would find out. But my need and desire to finally have an answer superseded any fears or concerns I had about what I would find out.

I was grateful for the doctor's information and called him immediately. Like many specialists, there was a 3 month wait before we could see him. I guess it was somewhat reassuring that he was in such high demand. If I could have had an appointment the next day, I may have wondered why a specialist's schedule was wide open.

Like the school district in Illinois, I was back to filling

out a variety of forms. There were so many questions on everything from my pregnancy, the delivery, and the first few years of Jason's life. The teachers also completed forms about Jason's interaction with the other children, his grasp of concepts, and overall behavior in the classroom. I waited patiently but was anxious for our initial visit.

During our visit, he asked me about the forms I completed and additional questions about our home routine. He wanted to know how Jason handled changes in his life and how he interacted with those around him. He then spent an extensive amount of time with Jason alone where I observed through a one-way mirror. He engaged him with a multitude of games, books, and questions in an attempt to determine what made Jason tick. Overall, Jason interacted well with the doctor, which was a huge relief. You never know if doctors can obtain the information they need to make a diagnosis but in this case, there were no problems.

We made a follow up appointment for two weeks later. This time, Jason was not joining me and the appointment was for parents only. As time got closer to our visit, I could feel myself becoming more apprehensive. I had no idea what they could tell me. But the day came and the time had finally arrived. As clear as day, I remember sitting in the doctor's office 14 years ago and him explaining to us his findings. My husband and I are both college educated people but what we were about to hear could never have prepared us for the diagnosis.

First, You Cry

We were told that Jason had PDD-NOS. This stood for Pervasive Developmental Disorder – Not Otherwise Specified. PDD-NOS is a subcategory of autism and our child was on the autism spectrum.

I remember thinking "What did he just say?" "He said that Jason had PDD what?" "He is on the Autism spectrum?" "What is he talking about?" I tried listening as intently as possible absorbing each word but had trouble grasping what he was trying to tell me. I had never heard of PDD-NOS. I had heard of autism but always thought it applied to a child who sits in a corner, rocking back and forth with no speech. I love the movies and remembered "Rain Man" with Dustin Hoffman several years prior. But Jason wasn't like Dustin Hoffman's character; he was much higher functioning than that.

I was in shock about what the doctor explained. It's not that I didn't believe him. He was highly regarded and an expert in diagnosing kids like Jason. I was just so confused. When I was in the delivery room, I didn't expect that 4 years later I would be seeing a specialist because my child's development was delayed.

The doctor was extremely patient and answered our questions with great care and compassion. I'm sure we asked the same questions repeatedly in our efforts to fully understand Jason's diagnosis. He gave us several articles to read that would answer many of our questions, a summary of his findings and several suggestions as to the best course of action to help Jason. He was a wealth of information and recommended special education schools, various therapies, and support groups that he hoped we would take advantage of. He was very kind and knew we were completely bewildered. I'm sure we were not the first set of parents that asked the same questions continually. I have no doubt we would not be the last.

Then, you cry. And you cry again. I distinctly remember driving home from the doctor's office and my husband and I just feeling so sad. We were committed more than ever to Jason and would do whatever it took to help him. We loved Jason so much – parents couldn't love a child more. But after hearing news like we did, your love takes on an even deeper meaning. Is that possible? I don't know for sure but I do believe that the parent/child bond can become even stronger when faced with these obstacles.

My husband called his parents and I called mine. We tried to explain as best we could what the doctor told us. It was hard enough for us to comprehend and to then explain it to our parents - this was a most difficult task. Moreover, with the difference in generations, they had less of an understanding about what we were talking about. Kids weren't given special labels years ago. They were lumped into a couple of categories and that was it. They didn't have the same diagnostic tests that are available today. They hadn't heard of PDD-NOS and their view of autism mirrored ours – a child sitting in a corner rocking back and forth with limited speech. They were as sad as we were to hear the news. Being devoted grandparents, they reassured us of their love for Jason and that nothing would ever change that.

I'd love to say that everything was business as usual when it came to all of us relating to him. I don't feel this was the case. There was this "walk on eggshells" feeling that we all had at first. What do you now expect from your child who you've been told has serious developmental delays? I was always an understanding mother and believed I was fair when it came to parenting. What should I do differently now? Should I be more stringent or less stringent? I knew that a routine and structure were important for any child but should I be less rigid? All of these questions and more were racing through my mind.

As I began reading the articles the doctor gave me, I cried again. In some ways, the material seemed foreign to me and in other ways it was as though the authors of these articles knew my child without ever having met him. It was surreal and overwhelming at the same time. I searched for every article and every resource imaginable to help me understand what Jason had. I was on a mission and nothing could stop me. You have to remember this was 1996 and there was not a lot of information about PDD-NOS. New information was emerging all the time but there was still so much the medical community did not know about Autism Spectrum Disorders.

Many years ago, doctors thought that autism and its related disorders were caused by poor parenting. I thank G-d that Jason was not diagnosed in the 1940s. At that time, autism was believed to be caused by cold, unloving mothers. They sometimes used the term "refrigerator mothers". Another renowned professor agreed and parents truly believed that they caused their child's autism. I could not imagine being told this by a doctor; it would be devastating for any parent to hear. The guilt these parents felt, especially the mothers, must have been horrendous. I don't fault the doctors, though, as this is what they truly believed at the time. I also don't believe there was malice involved or the doctors were looking for someone to blame. They just didn't know any better.

Each year, we find out more and more about many disorders and autism is no different. What we once believed one year can change a few years later, and then change again. It wasn't until the 1960s, where further research by doctors concluded that autism was not caused by cold parents. It is a biological disorder for which doctors believed there was no known cause or cure.

In researching all I could about autism, I learned that it was a social communication disorder that is genetically and neurologically based. Diagnosed cases of autism were on the rise and it is a spectrum disorder. A child falls somewhere on the spectrum from mild to moderate to severe. I wondered where my child fell on that spectrum. While I had hoped he was mild, I didn't know for sure and that was truly frightening. It's scary when your child is given a diagnosis and there is no pill he can take, no shot, nothing. It would have been easier if they told me to do x, y and z— then everything should be fine. Come back and see them in 6 months and we'll reevaluate. While the doctor offered special schools and therapies, the fear of the unknown was upsetting and that feeling never left me, even to this day. For me, it is one of the most painful aspects in dealing with this. None of us has a crystal ball and no one can predict the future but when it comes to development, it's even more of an enigma. You help your child progress and give them the necessary tools to do so. It's just you really don't know if and when they will reach a certain developmental stage.

I went to the PDD support group and found it helpful. Unfortunately, it was a bit of a distance from my home so it wasn't easy to socialize with the other parents outside of the meetings. At least it was a start and that was all I needed since we knew of no one whose child had special needs like ours. It was a very lonely and isolating feeling. We had wonderful friends who tried to comfort us but they didn't know much about the disorder either. They were sympathetic but couldn't relate to my daily challenges raising Jason. Moreover, as Jason got older, their children didn't understand. He was immature, wanted to play with toys or watch television shows that the other kids outgrew. Some of the kids would still want to have play dates with us but sadly, the list grew smaller and smaller. I was told this isn't unusual by the parents in my support group. People don't know what to say, how to act, and certainly had trouble explaining it to their children. And these kids were not even 5 years old – I could only imagine what it would be like when he's older.

We did finish out the year at the preschool he was in, as there were only a few months left. At least twice a week, there was an unusual story or incident that the teachers wanted to relay to me. They were not mean spirited in any way and did not want me to feel badly that these things happened. They just wanted me to be aware and I completely respected and appreciated their position. When I attended weekly parent/child activities at the school, I was very self conscious. It was now so obvious that my child was different from the other kids and the parents were really noticing it as well. I would often receive looks and Jason did too. I had a few close friends who always stood by me and were accepting of us. But for the many that were not, that was painful to deal with. I just tried to make it through each day until the end of the school year in May. As hard as it was to finish the year, I was just relieved I didn't have to switch him to a new school in the middle of the year. I feel that would have been a huge adjustment for any child and especially for him.

As I mentioned, the doctor recommended that Jason be enrolled in speech therapy again and also receive occupational therapy. I followed every suggestion and within a couple of weeks, he was evaluated and receiving both therapies twice a week. I don't have to explain the financial ramifications of this. While we had insurance and they covered some of it, they only covered so many visits and there were co-pays. The costs were exorbitant and it was a struggle. But this was my child and I had to do what it took to get him the help he needed. It was very time consuming and we were driving constantly to appointments. I felt very badly for Ryan because he was either in his car seat or in a waiting room while Jason was in therapy. It wasn't fair but there wasn't anything I could do about it.

Occasionally, I would have a sitter for Ryan so he could at least be at home playing with his toys or being taken for a walk in the stroller, but sitters were expensive too and I could only do this so often. I kept telling myself that I was doing the best I could but there was a nagging feeling of wondering if I was doing enough. When we were home, I tried as much as possible to play and interact with Ryan to make up for the time he spent running with me to different appointments. In addition to the speech and occupational therapy, I spent many hours researching special education schools – both private and within our public school system. This, too, was foreign to me as I had just moved to Houston and was learning my way around. Of course none of the schools were in my area; they were all 30 minutes or more away. It was very awkward for me to visit them. It's not that the staff at these schools was unwelcoming. On the contrary, they were understanding and answered all of my questions. All of this was just so new to me and after living in Houston for less than a year and now having to find another school was a daunting task.

I went on all of the tours and came with my list of questions. What was the teacher/student ratio? What degrees did the teachers have? How many years experience did they have? What made one school a better fit than the others? What was the maximum number of students in any given class? I was also concerned about role models for my child. When I observed the classes at each school, some of the kids were not well behaved. I fully realized that all of the kids were there for a reason and needed extra help. The worry was that he would pick up inappropriate behaviors since each of the kids had different levels of functioning.

While some were higher functioning and he could learn from them, it was the children with severe behavior issues that made me feel uneasy. I certainly didn't believe my child was better than these kids – not at all. He had his share of issues which was why we were there. I felt awful thinking that I didn't want Jason at any of these schools. I wanted him to stay with the typically developing kids at his current preschool. It is a tremendous loss when you plan on your child attending a certain school and then it changes.

I decided on sending him to a private school that had two teachers and 10 students per class. I felt this would be the best school and hoped it would be a great year ahead. The lead teacher had her Masters degree in speech pathology and I felt this would be beneficial in helping Jason develop his communication skills. Most of the other kids at the school had one form or another of a communication disorder. It was unbelievably costly to attend. Our saving grace was that we received a huge tax refund that year. It covered the entire tuition and was a blessing. The decision was made in March and I felt better that a plan was in place. He would begin his new program in August of 1996.

Even though he did not attend our local public school, he was still eligible to receive services through the district including speech therapy, occupational therapy, and an in-home trainer to work on social skills. We took advantage of these services and somehow managed to fit it all in during the school week. I was given an in-home program as well to further advance Jason's emerging skills. I was not a drill sergeant and was cognizant of the fact he had a long school day and long weeks in general. I made our learning time fun and only worked with him on the weekends. Granted, it was for 1 ½ - 2 hours at a time, but he was really fine with it. It was play time with Mom and we worked on everything from fine motor schools to gross motor skills and academics. Kids need their downtime and I made sure to keep it light but engaging. I made sure to schedule our time during Ryan's naps so I could focus on him during his waking hours.

At the same time, I started to notice Ryan often was often in his own world and lacked eye contact. He had just turned one year old and I could tell that something wasn't right. Like Jason at this age, he spoke only a few words and was only crawling. I was so much smarter about it this time and because of all of information I read about PDD-NOS, I knew what signs to look for. I called the same developmental pediatrician and they sent me another set of forms to complete. It was déjà vu and not even 6 months since I had filled out the same forms for Jason. I couldn't believe I was back to doing it again and scheduling an evaluation for Ryan but as the saying goes – it is what it is.

I'll never forget sitting in the examination room after the doctor had completed his diagnostic tests. He asked various questions about what I had written on the parent questionnaire. He nodded his head and asked more questions. I then asked that ever so frightening question. "You're going to tell me that Ryan is autistic also, aren't you?" He looked at me and said, "I'm so sorry".

Tears just rolled down my cheeks. Part of me sat there in disbelief and the other part of me just knew what he was going to say. It was as though I knew his answer before he told me. After all, I did make the appointment myself when Ryan had just turned a year old. There was no teacher telling me anything was wrong. Our new pediatrician could see that Ryan was delayed but didn't mention anything about having him tested further.

It was still strange and it started to feel like everything was in slow motion as all of these thoughts raced through my mind. How was I going to handle two children on the autism spectrum? Did Ryan need speech therapy? Occupational therapy? Did I do something wrong? Did I not spend enough time with him? Did this happen because I spend too much time with Jason? How were we going to afford another child with special needs? If I thought I was overwhelmed before, it was nothing like what life had in store for me from then on.

And Now There Are Two

It was very painful to tell family and friends that Ryan was on the autism spectrum, too. While the clinical diagnosis was again PDD-NOS – that term was still foreign to many. For me, it sank in right away that this was the hand I had been dealt. Yet coping with it all was unreal in so many ways. I truly couldn't believe what was happening but quickly dove into the task at hand of getting Ryan the help that he needed. Since he was only one year old, so much younger than Jason when he was diagnosed, the doctor's suggestions were much different this time. We were located in the Houston Independent School District and they had a program called Early Childhood Intervention (ECI). They evaluate children from birth to 3 years old and performed their own set of diagnostic tests. They also concluded that Ryan had PDD-NOS and wanted to help us.

It was a wonderful feeling knowing that these services were available. We had weekly visits from a speech therapist, occupational therapist and case manager who worked on cognitive skills and interactive play. They worked together as a team to create a home program I could work on with Ryan while they reinforced the techniques during their weekly visits. They became part of our family and I confided in them about my trials raising two children with special needs. It helped that I could talk openly with them and their caring about my well-being meant so much to me. It was obvious I was stretched to the limits.

As we were adjusting to Ryan's home visits and routine, Jason began his new school in August 1996. I was driving Jason to his special school, which was thirty minutes from our house when there wasn't any traffic. Fortunately, I was an organized person and planned ahead. This trait served me well and in the years to follow. We actually were able to form a carpool with another boy who lived only a few minutes away. This helped and Jason became friends with this boy. It was great for him to have a friend to play with and while they didn't always play well together, at least it was a friend for him. He was a very sweet boy and for the most part, they enjoyed being with each other.

Because Ryan was so young, there wasn't a special education school I could send him to at 13 months old. I continued with the in-home visits from the therapists from our school district. I wanted him in a pre-school program regardless of his diagnosis so he could be exposed to his peers and learn as much as possible. I visited a Child's Day Out (CDO) program at our local Jewish Community Center and I was very open about Ryan from the beginning, telling the program director everything about his diagnosis. I could not imagine keeping them in the dark and not being upfront about his developmental delays. They needed to make an informed decision. The school accepted him and felt he would be fine in their program. The good news is that it was only 5 minutes from our house. Had it been further, I think this would have put me over the edge. I was exhausted from driving Jason to his school part-time and adding another long drive would have been really stressful.

Ryan's teachers were incredible! They were supportive, loving, and worked very hard to teach him. He was not walking unassisted yet and technically, this was required to attend the CDO program. He still needed help and when you have a lot of kids in the class it's hard for teachers to focus on just one child. But they really were amazing and so patient. The director also monitored Ryan's progress because she had to make sure that the teachers were not overloaded. She was encouraging and wanted Ryan in the program, but she did have to look out for the other children in the class.

It was not until Ryan was 20 months old that he began to walk. His first time was actually at the school. The teachers were ecstatic – you would have thought Ryan was their child! That was fine with me, as I wanted teachers who truly cared about him. I had hit the jackpot and was grateful to have them in his life. But like many things in life, our ability to send Ryan to this school had to come to an end. As he was approaching the two year mark, our case manager told me of another school that could help Ryan. It was different than the school Jason went to. This school had a different approach to teaching children with communication disorders that he thought would work well. They had specialists in areas of pre-academics, language, sensory-motor and social/play skills. There were 5-6 children in a class with a teacher and a teacher's aide.

Like with Jason, it was very hard for me to transfer Ryan from one school to another. While I knew it was the best decision for him and the teachers at his new school could help him more, it was still another change. I knew in my heart I had to do it because I never shied away from doing what I felt in the best interest of my children and certainly wasn't going to now. His old teachers and I cried when we had to say goodbye; but they also knew that I was doing the right thing.

While I was preparing Ryan and myself for his new school, I was concerned about Jason and felt that he might need a different school as well. While I was pleased with his teachers and their teaching methods, I felt another school might be better suited for him the following school year. Jason was progressing and communicating much better, but we were concerned that not enough academics were being taught. We checked into another school where the other students didn't have just communication disorders. They had a variety of students with dyslexia and general learning delays. They typically took only one student with autism per class. Their program was more of an academic program and while they believed social skills were very important, they stressed academics more. It was difficult to choose the right school – to find a balance between the amount of academics they would teach and the amount of time that would be spent teaching social skills. Too much focus on one at the expense of the other was not optimal. As much as I hated having him go to yet another school, I had him switch in the fall of 1997.

Believe me, I questioned if this was the right decision. This would be the third school in three years. The first school we had to leave because of his diagnosis. The current school was the best match for that school year. His needs had changed and thus, I started the search for a new school. We were not asked to leave the school and left on very good terms. It was just time for a different school with a different approach.

The school year began; Ryan was becoming adjusted to his new school and Jason to his. Our morning routine was hectic to say the least. I would drive Jason to his school, still thirty minutes from our home, of course. I then drove almost another thirty minutes in the opposite direction so Ryan could attend his school. Fortunately, shortly into the school year, I was able to form a carpool for Jason and this helped quite a bit. It was still tiring and difficult to manage, but a few less trips a week did make a difference.

I would arrange for Ryan's therapists in the afternoon when he got home from his morning program but before Jason came home from school. When I look back, it was a lot but this was the schedule. I was grateful the schools were available. If we lived in a small town with limited resources, neither child would have progressed as much as they had.

Our lives were moving along. Ryan had wonderful teachers who again, were nurturing and warm. Jason's teacher was amazing – we loved her right away! She was firm but gentle with Jason and enjoyed having him in her class. There were five students in each class. At recess, they merged with the kids one year ahead of them. This was an important time for socialization and a break from the intense schedule.

Jason was just beginning to read and this was very exciting for all of us. At first, the teacher wasn't sure of his reading capabilities as Jason had trouble crossing mid-line. He would start to read a sentence and, halfway through the page, would stop as though it was the end. With practice, he learned to read all the way across the line to the right side of the page. We were on our way and were thrilled he achieved this milestone. I loved having him read to us – it was music to my ears. He would read for hours, but that was fine with me. Sure, it was extreme. But when you once wondered if your child would read at all, you don't care that they want to do it all the time.

As much as we loved his teacher, there were conflicts with a couple of kids at the school. This was extremely troubling for us because Jason was bothered tremendously. I know that kids have their differences and have to work them out on their own sometimes. But kids like Jason have trouble with this because social skills and communicating are his biggest deficits. Recess became a huge issue because interacting with the other kids was not happening in a positive way.

When he was at home, he would perseverate over what happened at school to the point it kept him up at night. I discussed the problems with the teachers many times and they tried to work with the other students and stressed interacting in a nicer way with their classmates. Jason was the rule police and if one of the kids did something they shouldn't have, he would tell the teacher. He truly believed he was doing the right thing because students should always do what the teacher says – no exceptions! This did not help and with a couple of the kids being bullies, the situation went from bad to worse. While I was thrilled he was thriving academically, his self-esteem was plummeting. It didn't matter to me if Jason was brilliant because he wasn't happy going to school and uncomfortable with his classmates. This was too high of a price to pay. I had to do something.

I realize you might be thinking – "What – you're sending him to another school?" I know. This would be the 4th school in 4 years. I couldn't believe it myself. How could this be happening again? Was I doing something wrong? Was I making it worse for Jason? Was I not letting him form relationships because he moved every year? My confidence as a parent was definitely in question and this was a very difficult time for me. I ached for Jason and couldn't bear to have him so unhappy. He wasn't acting spoiled or being difficult; he was sincerely bothered by a couple of kids in the class and could not get past it. These kids were not leaving the school so I had to make sure Jason did.

So the search for yet another school began! I was venting to the director at Ryan's school about my dilemma. Ryan was thriving in her program and I respected her opinion tremendously. She, too, was bothered about Jason's lack of self-esteem and knew it was important to address. She let me know that her school was opening a first time class for 1st graders and that she would love to have Jason in the class. Yes, it was a risk being in the inaugural class at any school because there are always kinks to work out. But she was confident her staff could improve his self-esteem so that he would be emotionally whole again. They were teaching the 1st grade curriculum from the school district and assured us it would be followed.

The decision was made and in August 1998, Jason started at yet another new school. He was very happy to leave the other school because he was at such a low point. It truly broke my heart that he felt that way; I was relieved to find him a new school where he would have the potential to feel good again.

When we had our final parent/teacher conference at his existing school, the teacher felt very badly we were leaving. She truly had given it her all and loved having Jason in her class. She had been teaching for 20 years and tried everything to make it work with him. I believed her; she was wonderful and very sincere in her efforts. But it just wasn't meant to be and it was time to move on. I wished her only the best, as she did for us. I still run into her from time to time and love seeing her. She was a wonderful teacher who deeply cared for her students and their well being.

The school year ended and it couldn't have been soon enough for Jason. I never dreamt the year would have gone as it had. I could only hope and pray the next school year would be different.

Change, Change and More Change

Kids with autism need a lot of structure and typically do not handle change well. The irony of this chapter is that this year had more changes than the previous years combined. There was a new school for Jason, a new afternoon program for Ryan, and major changes within our family.

We all know that marriage can be difficult and in those stressful times, we work very hard to weather the storm. Having children can add to the stress but again, we try our best to work out the differences and keep the family together. I have always believed in the institution of marriage and, along with my husband, took my vows very seriously. When my marriage began to experience problems, I was very concerned about the effect it would have on our children. We both loved Jason and Ryan so much and our goal was to keep the family together. I truly thought that this would happen until Ryan graduated high school.

I am a huge proponent of counseling and sought help to find answers to make it work. I counseled with my Rabbi and wondered what G-d wanted me to do. I believed that everything happens for a reason and while we don't always know the answer, things turn out the way they are supposed to. I struggled terribly as to what to do because I was terrified of how Jason and Ryan would cope. While my Rabbi felt it would be noble for me to stay in the marriage, he was very troubled about how I would manage. I had been married 12 years and truly thought it would last forever. I'm sad to write that this was not the case. I filed for divorce in 1998; Jason was almost 7 years old and Ryan was just over 3 years old.

We told Jason that Mommy and Daddy loved him very, very much. That we had problems and we tried so hard to fix them. But the problems couldn't be fixed and we were going to live in separate places. We stressed many times that the problems had nothing to do with him or Ryan. This was truly one of the most heartbreaking moments of my life. We felt terrible telling Jason the family as he knew it was going to change. He had been through so much in his seven short years and now this.

The guilt I carried with me was enormous and I questioned if it would ever go away. We explained that he would regularly see his dad, and he would always be a major part of his life. My ex-husband rented an apartment only 10 minutes away which was comforting to Jason. I bought Jason his own calendar so he knew exactly when he would be with me and when he would be with his dad. It was challenging at times because of changing work schedules and meetings; this made it difficult to always follow the routine. I always made sure to convey all changes to Jason the minute I knew of them.

Ryan was less aware. Yes, he was over 3 years old but was developmentally like an 18 month old. I'm sure he realized that his dad was not living with us any longer but there was not the same verbal understanding that Jason had. I explained as best I could and as much as I believed he could comprehend why life was the way it was.

In the spring of 1999, we moved from the house we'd been living in. I really tried to speak of our new home in only positive terms. We moved to a house only two blocks away; it was a blessing to be able to rent a home in our existing neighborhood. It was a much smaller home than what we came from but the kids really seemed okay with it. I'd like to think this was really the case and that I wasn't just telling myself that to feel better. I know this was such a confusing time for them – I didn't minimize their stress at all. I'll never know what was truly going on in their minds at the time because even though we talked about their feelings constantly, I'm sure they were very torn as well. Even though my kids had developmental delays, they could still tell that their parents were not getting along. I was very protective of both kids and tried to shield them as much as possible. Even though the marriage did not work out, I only spoke of their dad in the best light.

For me, it was one of the most painful times in my life. There were so many days where I would barely have the energy to pick up the phone. I was feeling so down that my doctor prescribed anti-depressants. I am a huge proponent of anything that helps people make it through difficult periods in their life. Between counseling and medication, it took a couple of years before I started to feel whole again. I didn't date during my separation, it just wasn't for me. I actually waited until a year after my divorce was final before I had my first date. I wanted to give myself time to cope and heal with everything that had transpired. My goal was to just focus on my kids.

When the school year began, I made sure the school

was informed of the divorce and wanted them to be on the lookout for any changes in Ryan's behavior. Being a new school for Jason, they were just getting to know him and wouldn't notice if he was acting differently than before. I did want them to take note of any unusual comments or behaviors, though. They were very supportive and understanding as I knew they would be.

Though they both attended the same school, they were in separate physical locations. The younger kids had one building and the older kids were in another building about 20 minutes away. I worked there part time with the younger kids; it was wonderful to be able to see Ryan during the day as he transitioned from class to class.

Since he was 3 years old, the school district had an afternoon preschool program at our local public school. He was no longer eligible to have the speech therapist, occupational therapist and case manager visit our home. The next step was the Preschool Program for Children with Disabilities (PPCD). I took Ryan to visit a couple of times and he loved his teachers. Again, I was blessed to have devoted teachers who wanted Ryan to thrive and celebrated his every achievement. It worked out that he attended one program in the morning and another program in the afternoon. I felt awful that he had to eat lunch in the car but we didn't have a choice. The schedule was very hectic and I did a lot of driving. When I look back, it's amazing it all got done because it was so much back and forth. I went through a tank of gas every four days – it was insane.

It was all worth it because Jason was having a great year and his self-esteem was slowly improving. He was connecting with his classmates and I could see the difference. Words cannot express how relieved I felt that he was finally starting to feel good about himself again. I would go through a tank of gas every two days if it meant him getting back on track. Ryan's classes were going well also. It's amazing to me that he managed both programs every day, but he did. It just became the routine and that was all he knew.

Given all that they were still coping with from the changes of the previous year, I wanted them to enjoy going to school and be comfortable in their surroundings. I tried very hard to give them a life that was as normal as possible. I realize that when kids' parents are divorced and parents are switching their schools every year, you might wonder how I could even think their life could be remotely normal. But each year and each program was best for each child at the time. I can honestly say I have no regrets about any of the decisions I made. I would never recommend what I did for another parent – I only know that the decisions made were truly the best for them. You have to be an advocate for your child and not afraid to speak up. You must be their voice and always remember that if you're honest with yourself, you will know what makes your child tick.

About half way through the school year, I was told that our neighborhood public school was starting a self contained class for children with high functioning autism. Ryan would be too young for the class and was still in his preschool program. Jason was the perfect age as he would be entering the 2nd grade. So many thoughts were running through my mind. Could this really be true? Should I really consider switching him yet again? Was I crazy to think that all of these changes wouldn't have a detrimental effect on him? He was doing well, both academically and socially. How could I even think of moving him now? The class would have no more than 8 children with a special education teacher and an aide. The core subjects would be taught by their teacher and they'd have ancillary classes with the regular education children. The goal was to very slowly mainstream students like Jason with an aide to make sure he was adjusting well and grasping the material.

I met with the new teacher several times. I had her observe Jason at his existing school to ensure she felt he would be a good match for her program. Please don't think for a moment that I didn't agonize over this decision. A new program with no track record was not comforting. Yes, I did it the previous year with Jason entering the 1st grade and was very lucky. But I felt I had no choice at the time because he was so unhappy at his school. This time, he was doing well. Why would I want to risk upsetting him?

I can't describe how I knew this new program would be right for him – I just knew. It was that gut feeling that you get when there is instant chemistry with the teacher and you just know it's right. Because of the wonderful teachers he had in 1st grade, his self-esteem was back to normal. I felt that if I kept him at his current school because I was afraid of the change, it would not be in Jason's best interest. They understood why I made the decision I did and always kept the door open should Jason need to return.

So we made the move and it paid off immensely. The teachers were incredible and the kids in the class began to gel. Being on the autism spectrum, they were alike in so many ways yet so different because they each had their own strengths and challenges. The relief I felt knowing my instincts were correct in placing him in this class were indescribable. Jason could receive speech therapy, occupational therapy, and social skills training during his school day. It was a blessing and everyone worked together as a team. The therapists gave the teachers tips on how best to work with Jason and in turn, the teacher would make suggestions as to areas the therapists should focus on. This collaborative effort was instrumental in his growth and it showed.

As a class, they would participate in music, art and physical education with the mainstream classes. This allowed them to assimilate within the school. They also attended all school programs and special events; this inclusion was important and the teachers and school administration were in agreement on this. Another year was progressing and I was happy for Jason.

Ryan graduated to the next level of his preschool program and was moved to another school. I know this appears to be a lot for such a young child and even I wondered how the school district could expect a child to adapt to so much change. Like I did with Jason, I took risks and they worked out for the best. Each public school in my neighborhood was responsible for specific special education classes. I kept telling myself that this is the reality of my world and it is now Ryan's turn to attend the next school.

This time, some of his friends moved with him and it was so much easier. It was almost seamless because he already knew some of his classmates. There were kids he didn't know but the teacher had a wonderful ability to integrate the kids so that no one was excluded. She, too, had her degree in special education and had an aide to assist her. Ryan continued to attend his private preschool program in the morning and the public school program in the afternoon. My schedule was actually becoming easier because only the morning school was a distance from our home. Jason was at a school just a block from our house and Ryan's afternoon program was 5 minutes away. Life was good – it was very good, and I never took it for granted.

Jason's program was such a success that the school district decided to launch another self-contained class for children Ryan's age. I thought I was dreaming! Another program mirrored after Jason's once Ryan completed his existing program – I never thought it would happen but it did. They were going to start this class the following school year. He would already know some of his classmates because they would move with him. It was close to our house and no more private tuition payments! No more driving on the toll-way to send my child to school.

It was unreal that this was finally happening. We finished our last year with the private school in the morning and public school program in the afternoon. In 2001, I actually had both kids in public school programs within 10 minutes of our house. If you would have told me three years earlier that this was going to happen, I would have thought you were crazy. Fortunately, our school district saw the need for classes that serve high functioning kids with autism. We live in a massive school district in Houston. I was eternally grateful that the Southwest District in which I was located believed in these classes and had the fortitude to create them. It was not an easy decision for the regional coordinator. There are so many kids with special needs and every one of them deserves the best class designed for them. Given the school funding deficits, it's next to impossible to make this happen. With autism on the rise, they knew they had to do something. My family is blessed that they did!

Prelude to the Stories!

Up until now, I've only shared a few of the unusual stories about my kids. I wanted to focus on their early school years and for you to really understand the time, energy, and effort it took to find the right class each school year.

As I mentioned in the beginning, I have so many stories to tell you. My family and friends have told me for years that I need to write this book and share with others what my kids experience and how I help them through each day. I've always been a very realistic person and I call it like I see it and like I said in previous chapters – it is what it is. While I knew I had to accept my life as it was, there were so many days when I truly wondered if I was going to make it. Yes, I am a strong person but everyone has their limits. Through it all, one of the most important things I always tried to do was remain calm. Trust me; this was not an easy feat. It's very easy to yell when you're at the end of your rope and frustrated beyond belief. I'd be lying if I told you I didn't have some of those days and felt absolutely awful for acting that way. I knew that I was human but didn't want to be at times like this. I wanted to have the patience of Job at all times.

This isn't reality and when I did lose it, I was terrified of the long term effect this would have on my kids. I used to think then and even now "Great - that will be another six months worth of therapy when they're adults!" Honestly, this exact thought would run through my mind. It's that guilt that we feel as parents when we try to keep it together but just can't. People have told me for years how much patience I have. I often think that they don't know what goes on behind closed doors. In public, we all try to put on a great front as though we're in control and maintaining the peace. While I tell myself I've done the best I could – I know I am very hard on myself. It's my core personality and while I wish I were different – I am who I am.

While no two autistic children are alike, the actions they carry out and the words they speak are strikingly similar. The obsessions and quirks make them different than the rest of us but unique in their own way.

And the first group of stories is...

Hi, It's Nice to Meet You

The title of this chapter is an easy sentence, a standard greeting when you're introduced to someone for the first time. Or you could say "Hi, how are you?" This is nothing out of the ordinary and seems simple to most of us. This is not so with people on the autism spectrum. Remember that autism is a social communication disorder and manifests itself in different ways. One of the most prevalent is during basic conversation with others. When my kids were younger, I had to teach them over and over that when they meet someone for the first time, there are certain greetings that are appropriate. If they know the person or are reminded that they've met them before, other greetings apply. I can't begin to tell you how often we would talk about this before we went to someone's house or went out to run errands. You never know when you'll run into people and I always had to give them gentle reminders. I'm sure I sounded like a broken record but I didn't care. You have to constantly drill these things into their minds because that's what it takes to get the job done.

Kids with autism focus on the most unusual facts to memorize. They also believe that because they are interested in a certain subject that everyone around them must be as well.

Most of us have a filter in our brain that helps us regulate what we should say and when. Sure, kids will say things that are inappropriate and as a society we accept this. But as kids get older, society expects them to outgrow these behaviors. To this day, Ryan, who is 16 years old, continues to have difficulty in conversations with others. Jason used to have difficulty when he was younger but outgrew this with time and maturity.

What could be so unusual you might wonder? How would you answer or respond to the following:

- What's your favorite periodic element?

- Michigan beat Notre Dame 27-21

- "Dalmatians" is on sale March 19

- Watch Bugs and Daffy on Cartoon Saturday on Cartoon Network

- Watch the Powerpuff Girls at 4:30, followed by Samurai Jack

- 1-800-call-ATT

- Yesterday, I had Kool-Aid to drink

- Do you know the middle name of our 9th President?

- Did you see that episode of Suite Life of Zack and Cody?

- Who discovered hydrogen?

As you read through that list – keep in mind this happened on a daily basis. To clarify for you what my kids were really trying to ask or tell you:

+ Jason memorized the entire periodic table of elements – every one of them. He was fascinated by this and had his favorite elements, so he assumed you would, too. Some people knew what the periodic elements were and could name one, but didn't exactly view it as a favorite. Who has a favorite periodic element? There were a lot of people who had no clue what he was even asking. Either they didn't study chemistry in school or were so surprised when they were asked the question; it just didn't register as to what they should answer.

+ Michigan beat Notre Dame 27-21 – He loves everything to do with University of Michigan sports. His father and grandfather attended college there and it quickly became his favorite school, too. Jason is a walking sports statistician. He has an incredible memory at remembering sports scores, specific plays within a game and the players involved. He used to read the ESPN encyclopedia for pleasure. He is a veritable Bob Costas and could easily consider being a sports statistician for his career.

+ If there was a movie that piqued Ryan's interest, he couldn't wait until it came out on video and wanted to make sure you knew as well.
+ Doesn't everyone want to watch Bugs and Daffy and the Powerpuff Girls? Ryan thinks you do.

- Even if you don't have AT&T for phone service, my kids want you to have their number.

- Ryan wants you to know what he had to drink the previous day.

- Doesn't everyone want to know the middle name of our 9th President? In case you were really wondering, it was William Harrison and his middle name is Henry.

- Suite Life of Zack and Cody is a popular television show on The Disney Channel.

- Henry Cavendish, an Englishman, discovered hydrogen. Another unknown fact was that if he ever saw his servants, he would fire them.

What's even more confusing is that we teach our kids not to talk to strangers yet, on a daily basis we speak to people all the time who we don't know. What are kids on the spectrum supposed to think? When I'm at a grocery store and going through the checkout line, the cashier greets me with "Hi, how are you?" I reply back, yet my son knows I've never met them before. If I see that someone is having difficulty opening a door, I automatically want to help and start speaking to them as I offer assistance. Again, I have no idea who they are.

Mixed signals like this are gray areas. Autistic people think in black and white – concrete terms. Do you speak to strangers or don't you? As they became older, I could explain that at certain times it was acceptable to talk to strangers who were employees in places like supermarkets, clothing stores and restaurants. During the early years, it was much tougher to explain in a manner they could comprehend.

When Ryan was 10 years old, he went with me to the hair salon. As I was paying my bill, he came up to me and said "Look, I got a quarter!" He said "The man gave it to me!" I went over to the man who could not have been sweeter – he was someone's grandfather I imagine. He said that Ryan guessed which hand the quarter was in so he gave it to him. It was very innocent and I didn't want to hurt his feelings. Ryan then blurted out "My tongue is blue because I drank PowerAde!" The man just looked at him wondering why he just said that. I felt terrible but I had Ryan return the quarter. I explained to the man how kind it was giving Ryan the quarter but that I was trying to teach my son to not take anything from strangers. I apologized again, but was very torn. The man said he understood but I wonder if he just thought I was being an overprotective mother.

Another similar situation happened at the movies. Two seats from us were parents with their kids. Ryan says "Hi!" very loudly. The man looked at us strangely and said hello. He then says "My name is Ryan!" very enthusiastically. The man had a more puzzled look because then Ryan asked his name. The man replied, "My name is Bill." Ryan turned to me and said, "Mom, say hi to Bill." I quietly said hello and politely waved. Bill replied, "We have some extra candy that we didn't realize – would you like some?" Ryan would have taken it in a heartbeat but I said no thank you. Ryan told me, "See mom, they're not strangers – they wanted to give us candy." I thought I was going to die – it's every parent's nightmare that their child will be lured with candy. It's easy for any child to be taken advantage of. People with autism have a naïve quality about them that never really goes away. It lessens with age to some extent, but that naiveté will always be a part of them.

Closing conversations was another struggle and still is with Ryan. Most of us know that there are several ways to finish a conversation offering closure for both parties. A few examples are:

- It's nice to meet you, too
- Thank you
- Great to see you

Ryan would just walk away when he was finished with the conversation.

It didn't matter if he had answered the other person's question or if he asked a question and didn't wait for the answer. As he is often in his own world and is in many ways egocentric, he will ignore his surroundings. You can't imagine the number of times I've worked with him on this through role playing and correcting him in public. He has improved but has a long way to go and because he is 16 years old, it makes him stand out even more. As a parent, you have to keep at it until it really sinks in.

Another crucial aspect of social conversation is eye contact. During conversation, looking someone in the eye while you're speaking to them or vice versa conveys the message that you want to be engaged in the conversation. It shows that you are interested in what is being communicated and allows for that back and forth banter. Granted, when we're talking and thinking through our thoughts out loud we may glance away. But our eye contact resumes after that brief pause. This is not the case many times with autistic children and adults.

I don't believe it's a conscious decision to act like you're ignoring someone. I've had some kids tell me that it actually hurts when they look someone straight in the eye. This may sound farfetched to some of you but I honestly believe that it is difficult for them. They can't explain why it hurts; it just does.

For others, we don't know why that lack of eye contact exists. It's one of the first clues for me when I suspect someone is on the autism spectrum; I can spot it a mile away and so can a few of my friends whose kids are on it too. We just know and accept it for what it is. Sadly, most people don't understand why someone doesn't look at them during a conversation and believe they are very strange for doing this. I wish that when my kids do this that I could explain to the other person why this is happening. But I can't be everywhere and explain to every person the issues they have to cope with. It is part of that breaking away that all parents experience and allow your kids to be their own person in their own way. As I've said before, with my kids, it's more extreme and so very complicated. Like other parents, I hope and pray for the best.

What are you trying to tell me? Please be specific!

In addition to grasping those conversation skills, many people with autism don't understand sarcasm, jokes or euphemisms. People with autism are very concrete thinkers. So many people do not understand this and when they're attempting to communicate with someone on the autism spectrum, the conversation is completely lost because the person they're speaking with is confused. They may not express this confusion making you wonder even more where the conversation is going. It's not until it's gotten entirely out of hand that you may realize you need to speak in more specific terms.

Communication for my kids can be so foggy at times. I have to be extremely careful of the words I choose and just when I think I've been, I've confused one of my kids and have to clarify what I'm trying to tell them. Trying to explain this to those around them is most trying. Most of us don't need such clarity in a conversation. We can interpret what someone is trying to tell us and draw conclusions. Not my kids, that's next to impossible. It could be as simple as:

- When I'd tell Jason that I'd drop him off at his friend's house, Ryan would burst into tears. I had no idea why he was crying. I'd ask him what was wrong and he'd tell me, "Don't drop Jason." He actually thought I was going to pick Jason up in the air and physically drop him at his friend's house.

- Jason was mainstreamed for a couple of classes in elementary school. When I met his math teacher, she told me that Jason was a "wonderful addition to her class". Jason was standing beside me and I just knew he didn't know what she meant. When I asked him, he started adding numbers. She said "addition" and when he hears that, he begins to add numbers in his head. He didn't make the connection that addition could be used in a different context.

- A friend called me one day to tell me that she felt terrible about what had happened while Jason was playing at her house. My son was playing with her son and everything was going fine. They had played together many times so I knew what transpired couldn't have been that bad. She realized her son had gotten into something he shouldn't have and she was really angry. She said to her child, "If you touch that again, I'm going to kill you!" A few minutes later, my son went up to her and asked, "Where is your gun?" She explained that she didn't have a gun in her house and she never would. He told her that she said she was going to kill her son. She realized why he was confused and tried to explain what she meant and that it was just an expression. Eventually he understood but initially he was worried she had a gun and was going to use it.

- One of my friends was joking one day and said he had won a million dollars. My kid believed him and began asking how he won it. I explained that our friend did not win all that money. He didn't understand why he said it if it wasn't true. He couldn't understand why someone would joke about something like that.

- Putting Ryan to bed one night, it came out that a kid at school told him he had a million dollars. Considering this kid was only in 5th grade, I knew this was highly unlikely. I asked Ryan, "What do you think? Do you think your friend has a million dollars?" He said he didn't know and asked if I thought it was true. I wanted Ryan to tell me his thoughts first so I could see what he was thinking. Moments like this are teachable ones. As a parent, I can't help him unless I understand his thought process. He told me that his friend was honest so it must be true. Clearly, I had some teaching to do.

- Many years ago, I used to work in a catering department of a specialty store. My general manager had the last name of "Brown". When I introduced one of my kids to him, he asked me if he was Lee Brown's brother. At the time, Lee Brown was the mayor of Houston. Since my manager had the same last name as our mayor, he assumed they must be related.

- In the front of the specialty store where I worked, there was a banner that said, "By popular demand, new store hours 8am – 10pm!" My child asked, "Did they come up to you and demand? How did they know who to go to and demand what they wanted?" His confusion began because at his age, you don't demand anything. When he saw popular and demand in the same sentence, it made no sense to him. I explained that people suggested the store be kept open longer. Popular demand is just an expression.

- When Ryan was 7 years old, I picked him up from Sunday school one day. I offered him an apple, one of his usual snacks. He told me he would no longer eat apples. I knew there must be a reason he was thinking this way but he had trouble explaining why. Since he had just gotten home, I put two together and had a feeling it had something to do with what they talked about. I was able to call the teacher at home and asked him what they discussed in class. He explained they were reviewing the story of Adam and Eve. It quickly made sense to me why he wouldn't eat apples any longer. I tried to clarify several times that it was fine for him to eat apples. I even had the teacher speak to him and offer reassurance. It took him 3 days before he would eat another apple.

- At school, Jason had to read a story and answer questions. The characters in the story were named

Judy and Jim. He said, "My dad isn't named Jim. They made a mistake." The teacher had to explain the story was not about his parents. There are thousands of people named Judy and Jim; the author was not talking about his family. He continued to read the story and questioned the teacher again. She explained the author just chose these two names for no special reason. As he continued reading the story, it said, "Judy eats a lot of junk food and doesn't exercise". My child told his teacher, "My mom doesn't eat a lot of junk food but it's true, she doesn't exercise." Clearly, he thought the story was still about his parents.

+ A new restaurant was opening in our neighborhood. Ryan said he couldn't wait to go, he knew it would be a great place. I asked him how he was so sure. He told me that the sign in front of the restaurant said "Good Food and Fun". The sign told him, so it had to be true.

+ Ryan loves fast food – he is the fast food king. When one of the chain restaurants came out with Chicken Fries, he was very excited. The commercial told him these were made out of chicken and he didn't question it. When my mom took him through the drive through, he saw onion rings and asked her what they were made of. She told him they were made of onions but he didn't believe her. After all, how can you tell what French fries are made of? They're not called potato fries. In his efforts to find out what onion rings are made of, he just had to ask the person at the window. I'm sure they wondered why he was asking.

+ Another time while in the drive through, my boyfriend was placing the usual order for Ryan – two cheeseburgers with ketchup and pickles and a large French fry. By accident, my boyfriend said ketchup and "pickle"; he didn't say "pickles". Ryan became hysterical, screaming that if you tell them pickle, they'd give you just one. You have to say pickles to get more than one.

+ When Ryan was 15, he asked me whether he would catch pneumonia if he got water on his skin. Clearly, he misunderstood something he was told at school and I explained that this was not how you caught it.

+ At a local restaurant, one of my kids went to the fountain machine and they were out of the soda he wanted. He said to his friend that it was weird they were out. The friend explained that they were just out of the syrup to make the soda – they weren't out of it permanently. My child thought that once the restaurant was out of it, that was it and there was no more. Forever!

+ At a friend's house one evening, the mom told the kids to get in her car. My child couldn't figure out what she was trying to tell him. When he went out into the driveway, her car was blocked in by another car. Why did she want him to get in her car when she couldn't get out of the driveway? He went back inside and asked her again and she confirmed to get in her car. She realized why he was confused and explained that they would move the other car first so that she could back her car out to leave. He couldn't think of that next step to move one car so the other car could leave the driveway.

All of the above examples illustrate how perplexing the world is to people with autism. We often take for granted the simplest things and assume the rest of the world understands as we do. And when a person with autism gives you that "deer in the headlights" look, they truly are attempting to gauge their surroundings. As you will learn in the next chapter, they may also exhibit some unusual habits as their ways of coping with their world.

Why is he doing that?

We will never know what goes on inside the mind of a person with autism. We can guess, attempt to interpret, and draw conclusions as to what we believe they are thinking, but none of us knows for sure and we don't know why they do the things they do. People with autism can display very unusual behaviors that those around them don't understand. Some behaviors occur because they have difficulty in verbalizing what they want. Other times, they have trouble understanding the world around them or become overwhelmed because of sensory overload. I know that it looks so strange when Ryan is in public and he expresses himself differently than the rest of us would. But I knew why he was acting in a certain way and truly believe that it's his way of coping with his surroundings. He's not acting this way to get attention or to intentionally misbehave. He's simply doing it because he has to in order to manage his way through this world.

A friend of mine has a child with Tourette's Syndrome, another disorder that our society often misunderstands and can be unsympathetic toward. Tourette's is an inherited neurological disorder with onset in childhood. There can be multiple physical tics and usually at least one vocal tic. The tics can wax and wane through the years with some being mild and some quite severe. Tourette's can last a lifetime but most people experience the worst symptoms in their early teens. Typically, the symptoms subside by their late teens and into adulthood. While neither of my kids was diagnosed with Tourette's, they've had their share of tics through the years. I know plenty of kids on the autism spectrum who did not experience this; we were not as fortunate. When speaking with our neurologist during their pre-teen years, he diagnosed each of them with a tic disorder. It's something we've just coped with through the years and dealt with as best we could. I did not give either of them medication because when these tics were at their height, the kids were on medication for ADD or anxiety. There are pharmacological ramifications when your child takes multiple medications and since the tics were somewhat manageable, the doctor did not prescribe any.

Did tics occur because of their autism or due to their tic disorders? We don't know for sure and in my opinion, I don't think it really matters. What I do know is that when we were out in public, it was very awkward because of the stares we have received in the past and continue to receive to this day. I don't know if my kids have ever been aware of this but I sure have been. It's so hard because I don't owe anyone an explanation. Logically, this makes sense; but emotionally, it's much more complex.

When Ryan was about 15 months old, he would bang his head on the floor. Since he wasn't verbal yet, it was his way of showing his frustration. Could he have been doing it to gain attention? Sure, I imagine this was the case at times. But for the most part, he was upset about something. It was so bad at times that he would have a red bump on his forehead. I tried many ways to get him to stop and worked with our case manager to curtail this behavior. At one point, I considered getting him a helmet out of concern for the potential damage to his skull.

One time, we were at a gathering for families with young children at our Temple. I was talking to one of the mothers when she noticed Ryan on the floor banging his head. She was worried I didn't know he was doing this and afraid he would hurt himself. I didn't think twice about it and told her he'd be fine, not to worry. She had this shocked look as I'm sure my attitude came across as cavalier. Realizing what I had done, I explained further why I wasn't running over to him. I knew he would be fine and eventually stop hurting himself. There was this need to explain myself.

I have often felt this way. In talking to other parents, they do the same thing. We know we don't have to justify what we do. On the other hand, we don't want to be perceived as parents who don't care about the welfare of our children or that we don't know how to discipline them. Once I clarified to my friend what I was doing and why, she felt much better. As far as the other 100+ people in the room who saw him and wondered why I didn't react, well…. I couldn't explain to everyone. I knew what they were thinking and I had to accept the situation for what it was. Fortunately, after several months, Ryan stopped this behavior, which could not have been soon enough for me.

Some autistic kids often flap their hands. They do this when they're excited, over stimulated, or anxious. Jason didn't exhibit this behavior but Ryan began when he was a toddler and continues to this day. He'll bounce up and down in place and his hands will flap away. I know parents who tell their kids to stop doing it and believe their child can control himself. I did go through a brief phase where I would gently put my hands on his shoulders to calm his body down. It usually helped for a few minutes but then he was back to bouncing and flapping. I can't speak for others, but I believe Ryan couldn't control himself and needed to do this because of feeling a certain way. Again, I'll never know for sure and don't think he even knows. At 16 years old, he continues these gestures and it is my hope that he won't still be doing them in his adult years.

Chewing on shirts. Yes, you're reading this correctly. Ryan used to chew on the collars of his t-shirts. He couldn't tell me why he was doing it but like most of his habits, they typically stemmed from stress. He would suck on the shirt for hours. You would have thought the shirt had been doused in water. The collar would get stretched out and when I washed it, it would only sometimes return to its original shape. Over time, running them through the dryer didn't work anymore. Ryan had sucked and pulled on them so hard, they completely lost their shapes. Some of the shirts had holes in them which I definitely couldn't fix. This phase took place mainly in elementary school. Needless to say, we went through a lot of t-shirts. Once in a while, he'll start up again, but for the most part it has subsided.

Another habit that Ryan displays is pacing back and forth. He doesn't do this at school but does it frequently at home and in restaurants. Out of the blue, he'll stop what he's doing and just start pacing. Sometimes this is accompanied by bouncing and hand flapping, which garners us even more looks when we're out in public. For the most part, I can honestly say it doesn't bother me anymore and I imagine it's because I'm used to it. When I'm with friends or family, I think they can feel uncomfortable and while I feel badly for them, Ryan is who he is.

I'll never forget one time when we were going to one of our favorite Houston restaurants, Carrabba's. I had taken the kids many times and they loved it. I tried to be very respectful of any establishment and bring Ryan during non-peak hours. I would never have wanted his pacing or bouncing up and down to cause problems for the wait staff and customers, or for Ryan to be hurt while they were serving food.

Normally, Carrabba's doesn't take reservations, but since we were a large party, we were able to make one early enough in the evening. It was a special night, my mom was flying in. Unfortunately, her plane was late, pushing our meeting time to much later. When I called to apologize and cancel the reservation, I explained my son had special needs. I was concerned he would be disruptive during their peak time. She asked me to please keep the reservation. They would seat us at a table in a corner so Ryan could move around if needed.

I was shocked that they would go to such great lengths to accommodate us. I started crying because I was so surprised at her level of compassion and how they went above and beyond. When we arrived, I thanked them profusely. I explained that my kids were autistic and their disability wasn't something you could necessarily see. Here I was explaining to strangers because I was concerned they may not believe that my kids really had special needs. I know other parents in my shoes that also tend to explain or justify because autism is so misunderstood.

The next day, I actually e-mailed Johnny Carrabba, their President, and complimented him on his hostess, manager, and establishment. It meant the world to me how his staff expressed such compassion for me and my family.

If everyone was like this, the world would truly be a kinder place. A few days later, Johnny actually called me. I was in disbelief when he identified himself on the phone. He wanted to thank me for writing such a beautiful letter and letting him know how wonderful his staff was. I couldn't believe he would take the time to reach out to me and will never forget my experience with them.

Even today, I'm careful when dining out. Whether it is a fast food place or casual dining restaurant, I try to place Ryan in a spot where he can get up if he needs to. For whatever reason, he will suddenly stand up and start bouncing up and down in place. That's just him and I feel he will eventually outgrow it. I doubt when he's an adult that he'll be doing this and, while no one knows for sure, that's just my gut feeling.

Ryan has always been fascinated with animals. He is so precious and loves dogs. After much discussion, I've taught him that he must ask the owner if it's okay to pet their animal, as some dogs can be very aggressive or overly shy. We have a neighborhood bark park that we go to since we don't have a dog. It's great because Ryan gets to see and play with so many dogs at once. It's in a controlled environment that is fenced in and I'm always close by. Most parents of a 16-year-old kid wouldn't worry about such things, but I do. Ryan is emotionally like a 10 or 11-year-old. You wouldn't let a child that age off on their own. While Ryan is chronologically older, he's not mature at all.

We get very strange looks sometimes because people will ask which dog is ours. When we tell them we don't have one and we come and visit the bark park to get our dog fix, they give us a puzzled look but are still polite. It's so funny because Ryan can remember a dog's name from 3 months ago and he will go looking for that dog every time we return to the bark park. But when it comes to people, it takes forever for him to remember someone's name. I realize that we all remember what we believe is important to us; it just makes me laugh that Ryan remembers animals over people.

Ryan went through a very unusual stage when he was about 6 years old. He would bark just like a dog. I'm not kidding! I thought I would die when we were in a restaurant and he'd start barking. You can just imagine the looks we received. I'd quickly tell him to stop, but he would start up again. There would be consequences if he continued, and he finally got the point that this was not acceptable behavior. To him it was okay because he loved dogs so much and that was his way of showing it. Fortunately, that phase lasted only a few months.

The phase returned when he was 11 years old and he would crawl on the floor like a cat. He loves cats, too, and plays with them when he's at his dad's house. At the time, I managed a specialty café and he came to work with me. When he started crawling, I immediately told him to stop. There was a customer nearby and I apologized to her for him doing this in the restaurant. She was very nice and said "Don't worry, I have an 8-year-old and understand." I didn't have the heart to tell her he was over 11 years old.

Through the years, both kids have gone through long phases of either clearing their throat or making gulping noises. I know they don't mean to do it or even realize what they're doing. It's just part of their tic disorder. Keep in mind that the disorder itself never goes away; the tics are just replaced by something else. They may go through a period of not exhibiting any tics but then the tics will resurface.

You never know what the tic will be or when it will recur.

In middle school, Ryan was clearing his throat so much that it was disturbing the other kids in the class. I felt terrible but there was nothing I could do. My heart broke for Ryan because I knew the kids teased him and I don't think he really understood why. It wasn't anything intentional; that was just Ryan at that point in his life. I was blessed that the teachers were very compassionate and did the best they could to work with his classmates to be more understanding of him.

I don't think people realize the great lengths that parents like me go to when we go to public places. It's not that I am afraid. But if we're in a movie theatre and Ryan is constantly clearing his throat or making gulping sounds, I feel badly for those around us. Yes, we've had plenty of looks. Fortunately, the people next to us continue to watch the movie and either get used to it or realize he can't help it. With the movies, I try to sit where there is an empty seat between Ryan and the next person. If we're going with friends, I'll try to put him in the middle if I think the people we're with won't be bothered by his noises. Sometimes this isn't possible and the movie theatre is packed. In cases like that, I just manage the best I can and pray we don't disturb the other patrons.

Something that I don't believe he'll outgrow anytime soon is his constant need to wash his hands. He will typically wash his hands three times while we're at a restaurant. This doesn't faze me now because he can go to the bathroom by himself and I can watch where he's going. But when he was younger, it was a bit disruptive because I would always have to go with him. This is just part of his obsessive-compulsive disorder (OCD) and part of his personality. I don't believe the OCD will ever go away completely; it will always be a part of him, more severe at times and always unpredictable. My family and close friends are used to this behavior but when we're around new people, they ask me why he keeps getting up and wondering if he is okay. I explain he's fine and what he's doing is just part of who he is.

One of the most painful periods of our lives was during the period when Ryan would pull out his eyelashes and hair. At first, I noticed that he was pulling his eyelashes and was very concerned. I then noticed bald spots on his head. The condition is called Trichotillomania with the peak age of onset between 9 and 13. Ryan was 11 and I was not prepared for this part of our lives. If the problem had stopped with his eyelashes, it would have been somewhat controllable and some people didn't even notice. When he began pulling out his hair in tiny patches, I could brush his hair a certain way in an attempt to cover it up. At the height of his hair pulling, there was a strip about three inches wide stretching from the top of his head to his forehead. It was frightening. School rules didn't allow kids to wear hats in class but they made an exception for Ryan.

I tried everything possible in hopes of helping him. I contacted the national help center for Trichotillomania to see if they had any suggestions. I e-mailed experts about the disorder hoping they could help me help Ryan. We tried giving him rubber bands to play with and every time he wanted to pull out his eyelashes or hair, he could pull on the rubber band. We tried stress balls and other manipulative toys that might be an outlet for him when he had the urge. Unfortunately, nothing worked and this lasted for about four months. The medical community hasn't determined if this disorder should be classified as an impulse control disorder, tic disorder, or put it under the obsessive-compulsive umbrella. To me, it doesn't matter what you call it because they're just labels. What's paramount is how you survive and manage day-to-day while nurturing those coping skills within your child. Needless to say, it was a very long four months while Ryan went through this phase. I was very relieved when this behavior subsided greatly.

Pulling out his hair never went away completely. As I've mentioned before, my kids were never "cured" of any of their behaviors. The manifestations of being impulsive or compulsive were always present; they were just replaced by new ones.

Now that Ryan is 16 years old, he is picking at his skin on the side of his face. This is called compulsive skin picking. It terrifies me as I write this; I am filled with fear and sadness. The behavior is believed to be triggered by stress. I have asked myself "Am I causing Ryan's stress?" Is there something at school causing the stress? I would be crushed if my actions were causing him to do this to himself. To most people, they probably think it's just your typical acne but I know this is not the case. I will keep a close eye and pray it can be controlled.

While attempting to find a balance between adding additional stresses to his life and making changes to bring Ryan out of his shell, I'm enrolling him in different programs and he is very unhappy that I am doing this. He prefers coming home from school every day and watching his television shows and playing his video games. This is fine, but only up to a point. The amount of time he spends in front of the television or playing video games is extreme. I believe it's important to expose him to activities where he can be with other kids, but not stress him out in the process. These last several months he is exerting independence more and more and is opposed to participating in these activities. I know this oppositional behavior is part of his growth as a teenager and typical for kids his age. The balancing act during this part of my parenting journey becomes more difficult because of my fear of putting too much pressure on him to try these new activities.

When I titled this chapter "Why is he doing that?", it was never my intention to have an answer for you. I don't know if there will be an answer in my lifetime. I chose this title because I am often asked this question by those around me. These disorders are extremely complex and no one can predict if there will be a cure. I wanted to help you understand that these behaviors are exhibited because they can't help it and this is who they are. It is my hope I have accomplished this.

Socks, Rituals and Obsessions

- Going to bed at 7:58 or 8:01. Not 8:00 or 8:05

- If given a time out, having them in increments of 5 minutes

- If asked the time, you can't reply with, "A little after 9:00," without being asked, "No, what time is it?" You have to tell the exact time.

- Having a sandwich cut into six pieces

- Drinking a glass of water with only two ice cubes

- Making sure there are six ketchup packets with your French fries

- If you're ordering a chicken sandwich with BBQ sauce, then you have to have two packets of BBQ sauce for your French fries instead of the ketchup

- At least two pickles on your cheeseburger

+ Only eating cheese pizza or pepperoni pizza with no pizza sauce

+ Playing basketball outside until you reach a certain score – no matter how long it takes and regardless of the weather conditions

+ Wearing three watches at the same time – one displaying Houston time, one for Eastern time, and the last watch for atomic time

+ Do not play more than two games of bowling at one time

+ Closing the car door three times or more until it makes a certain sound

+ When going through the drive through at the bank, you have to go in the same lane each time for each visit

+ Snapping your jeans multiple times until they make a certain sound

+ Not wearing a shirt because the button does not fit inside the hole the way you think it should

+ Tapping your hand three times on an object

What do the above statements have in common? They are all rituals my kids have lived by through the years. Trust me, there are even more but this list gives you an idea of our daily life. I love my kids so much, but this part of their personalities is exhausting. Crisis doesn't begin to describe what happens when their routine is altered. I call them meltdowns. Their world seems to crumble and they completely fall apart. Please don't confuse this behavior with a temper tantrum. They're not acting this way because they are spoiled or being selfish. They're acting this way because they desperately and truly believe this is how their worlds should be. In THEIR minds, it must be this way and when it isn't, it's catastrophic. While it doesn't have to make sense to you or me, it's what makes sense in the mind of a person with autism.

Most of us can be reasoned with. And sometimes my kids can be, too. As they are older now, I can occasionally give them a reason for something that they accept. But at other times, I can't reason or explain my way through it. There is no changing their minds. This is one of the many differences between typically developing kids and children with autism.

It is that extreme behavior that is crippling. When you can't leave the house in the morning because your jeans have to make a certain sound when you snap the button, a button has to fit inside the hole on your shirt a specific way, or a door has to shut "just so" before you can leave the garage – that's debilitating.

If you noticed, part of the title of this chapter is "socks". You would be shocked at Ryan's obsession regarding socks. Like many moms, I buy whatever socks are on sale because kids wear them out so quickly. Did you know that boys' socks come in the following styles?

+ Solid white with the brand name at the toe – in blue, red or black

- White with a reinforced toe and the brand name in red

- White with a reinforced toe and the brand name in blue

- The reinforced toe could be light gray or dark gray

- The sock may have a stripe (either red or blue) where the toe is reinforced

- Crew cut socks can fit more mid-calf versus the lower part of the calf

- The reinforced section can be larger in size covering more of the sock

I'll bet you didn't know about all of these little intricacies about socks. I didn't either until Ryan made me painfully aware. I swear I wash all of the socks at the same time. But somehow, they get lost or eaten by the dryer. Matching socks can be quite an ordeal because they MUST be exact in color and length. If they're not, our morning is not off to a good start. I realize that all kids have certain quirks. They fold their socks over a certain way or tie their shoes in a specific fashion. We all have habits like this. But when the habit takes over and you can't move past it, that's extreme and that is my world.

Getting Ryan out the door in the morning has gotten a lot easier because we have the routine in place. But it can still be time consuming and unpredictable because you never know when something will set him off. He could wear blue jeans one week and if they fit differently the following week, he has to know why. I explain that maybe they've shrunk a little or he could have grown slightly. To me, this makes sense. To Ryan, he wants everything to be the same and when it isn't, his world is rocked.

When he tucks in his shirt, we have the same problem. Sometimes there is more material to tuck in and sometimes there is less. I explain that shirts are made differently and some are longer in size. Therefore, there is more to tuck inside of his jeans. Ryan doesn't like this. He wants to tuck the same amount of t-shirt inside his jeans each time.

One of the most difficult dilemmas we face is when it comes to buying new shoes. When he was a toddler, this wasn't an issue. As he grew older, he was devastated if the shoe store didn't have the same exact shoe in the next size. I learned early on that if Ryan liked a certain style shoe, I should buy the next two sizes so we would have them once he outgrew the existing size. Manufacturers often change styles and by the time we were ready for the next size, our shoe style was no longer available. So I learned to stock up on the shoes to prevent these meltdowns. We had many painful times at the shoe store before I realized the need to do this. There were tears and sadness every time and we'd visit multiple stores to find just the right shoe.

Now the only problem is when it comes to dress shoes. Ryan hates wearing them because they're not his usual sneakers. To some extent, I can reason with him now that he's older and occasions arise when dress shoes are called for. But he doesn't like the change and they certainly don't look or feel the same when you wear them. Furthermore, I don't buy the next size up because he wears these shoes so infrequently that it's hard to predict when and what size he'll need in the future.

We have food and daily hygiene rituals as well. Ryan loves BBQ sauce so I make sure to have extra bottles in the pantry. The problem is that when there is about 20% of it left, he opens up a new bottle. I explain that I'm not going to just throw out the remainder and that he needs to finish the bottle. His concern is that it's almost finished and he doesn't want to run out. Dare I tell you that I have three open bottles of BBQ sauce in my refrigerator right now? He opens a new bottle when I'm not looking and hides it behind other bottles. I've explained that when he runs out, that's the time to open a new bottle and you don't waste the little bit that's left.

We have the same problem with shampoo bottles. He panics when it's running low and wants to open a new bottle. I've told him so many times that he has to finish the shampoo bottle he's currently using. I show him there is another bottle waiting for him to allay his concerns. Last week, he opened another bottle when I wasn't looking. Clearly, I have work to do in this department.

Most of us eat when we're hungry. We're flexible to some extent as to the time we eat and can eat breakfast food for supper and vice versa. If I ask Ryan at 10:30 what he wants for breakfast on a Saturday, he'll explain it's not breakfast – it's brunch! He's very emphatic about this and corrects me every time. You can only eat breakfast food for breakfast or at brunch. With me, I can eat pizza for breakfast. If it's 5:30 or 6:00, he'll ask what's for dinner. Yet if I ask him if he's hungry, he could say no. I ask him why he needs to eat dinner if he's not hungry. His reply is, "Because it's dinner time!" It took awhile to explain that it's fine to eat scrambled eggs for dinner. He argued that this was a breakfast food and not eaten for dinner. I finally convinced him that it's perfectly fine, but this took quite some time.

Seasonal changes continue to be problematic for Ryan. A few weeks ago, he told me out of the blue, "Spring is coming!" I thanked him for telling me and had no clue as to why this was on his mind. A short time later, he told me he was hot and we should turn on the air conditioning. I told him it was going to turn cooler tonight and we didn't need to turn the air conditioning on. He explained to me again that spring is coming and it's going to be warmer. Now I know why he told me this before. I told him spring hadn't arrived yet and for now, no a/c was needed.

He doesn't like those mid-season changes when it's warm in the daytime and cooler at night. He likes the same temperature, preferably cooler ones, most of the time. The arguments we have over the temperature in the house are not fun. I love to keep my house cool, believe me. But not when it's dropping into the 50s at night time. This concept is confusing to Ryan.

When it comes to driving, Ryan will frequently tell me I'm going the wrong way. Normally, he takes the special education bus to school but on occasion, I will take him. If I drive a different route than the bus driver, he argues with me. In his mind, I am altering his routine. I should be taking the same route as his bus does. I explain there are multiple ways to drive to the same place. He's much better about it now, but when he was younger he would become hysterical, thinking I had no idea how to take him to school. When we drive to restaurants or other familiar places, he'll argue with me again. It's wonderful that he's so aware of his surroundings, but frustrating because I know the roads better than he does. I will continue in my efforts to explain to him that in reaching any destination, you can take main streets, side streets and highways.

Going grocery shopping used to be quite an experience. When both kids were younger, they would be fixated on the packaging of their favorite food items. They knew the color, shape and pictures on the carton or bottle. It was embedded in their brains. The good news was that they could find what they wanted very quickly. This was most helpful especially when we were in a hurry. But what happens when the manufacturer changes the packaging? Do they not realize the ramifications of their actions when it comes to shopping for my children?

Obviously, manufacturers are always looking for new ways to promote their products. To me, this makes logical sense. We went through a period when the worst words in our vocabulary were "new and improved." Those words were the kiss of death for me. My kids could not understand why anyone would want to change a product or how you package it. What could be new about it? Why would you improve it? It was fine just the way it was and there was no need to change it. When they asked me why, I attempted to explain that the people who make these things want to try and make it better so that more customers will like it. I don't think I need to tell you that this explanation did not go over well. My kids could have cared less about the other customers. They only knew what was acceptable in their minds.

The rituals extend to their conversations as well. Everything has to be spoken in its entirety and exactly as advertised. From about the ages of 4 – 13, my kids loved the movies. We would see the same movies two and three times. Some might think this excessive but it made them so happy! Most of us will recall a movie by its name only. But when some of these movies are advertised, the studio advertises the star or presenter of the movie. Ryan picked up on this and when "The Santa Clause 2" came out, Ryan would tell people the movie is called "Tim Allen's – The Santa Clause 2". Another favorite movie shouldn't be called "Rugrats in Paris". It should be called "Rugrats in Paris – The Movie" because that's how it was advertised. In his mind, you were wrong unless you stated the complete name and he was the first to correct you.

Jason and Ryan would verbalize anything and everything that they were thinking. They obsessed over so many things. All kids do this when they're younger but most realize what is appropriate to verbalize as they get older. It took my kids a lot longer to grasp this concept and Ryan still has his moments even today. At any given moment, I was asked or told the following:

+ "Are you having problems with shampoo? Try Johnson and Johnson's new shampoo for dry hair."

+ "Did you know air purifiers can cure allergies and asthma? Try the new Ionic Breeze Air Purifier!"

+ "Have you tried the new Betty Crocker Deluxe Cake Maker? You can make wonderful cakes!"

+ "You should buy the Tempur-Pedic mattress for a great night's sleep!"

+ "We believe in people, we believe in you." Ryan started singing a song and I didn't recognize the tune or words at first. I knew it sounded familiar but couldn't place it at first. I then realized it was to a commercial for a local church here in Houston. This isn't something you expect your child to sing, especially when you don't even belong there.

- "Have you ever been shot?" When Jason began his fascination with history, he was a sponge and learned everything possible. In learning that one of our relatives had been shot in WWII, he would ask everyone if they had been shot before.

- "Do you know about the War of 1812?" Another popular question for Jason.

- "Do you like mittens?" This is a cat at his dad's house and Ryan would ask people this question. Clearly, they were clueless as to what he was talking about.

Ryan wants to buy every gadget or new product he sees. Some of these inventions really are great and occasionally, I will buy something. Having no concept of money or if something is expensive is not on Ryan's radar screen. When I attempt to explain, he used to reply, "Call Jim Adler, he'll get you money." I had to laugh. Jim Adler is a lawyer who advertises on television how he can help his clients and get them money. I explained I don't need a lawyer but again, the thought went right over his head.

My mom used to live in Michigan and usually came to visit us in March, July and December. We wanted to spread out her visits and considering her work schedule, these were the best months. Ryan became used to this and one year, she came in June. Ryan actually told her, "No, you can't come then. You come in July." The change was too dramatic for him. Of course Ryan does not dictate the schedule and my mom came in June, but it was a major adjustment for him.

All of these rituals come and go. You never know what new ritual will arise, what causes it or how long it will last. You just deal with them as best you can and hope they pass soon and don't cause too many problems. Rituals and obsessions are like a thunderstorm, you can't prevent them from occurring.

Speaking of the weather…

Fears and the Rule Police

In my world, fear and a need to follow rules are linked in so many ways. Because both kids are the Rule Police, they can be overcome with fear if they break the rules. This applies to every aspect of their lives. They are also very set in their ways and this lack of openness to change further fuels the anxiety. Now that Jason is 19 he has worked through a lot of his fears, which makes me so proud of him!

When he was as young as seven years old, his fear of thunderstorms and flooding caused a tremendous amount of anxiety in our lives. If we were at home during downpours, he was afraid that our house would be flooded and that we wouldn't be able to get out. Also on his mind was the fear that all of his treasured games and belongings would be ruined. Of course, it's frightening when the streets become flooded and the water is creeping up your driveway. I explained SO many times that we would be fine. But my efforts to constantly reassure him were not enough. I then had to explain that our house was not located within a flood zone. But as a precaution, we did have flood insurance just in case our home did flood. I had to further explain how insurance works in the event of flood damage. At his age, I shouldn't have been explaining flood zones and educating him about insurance policies. This is what it took to allay his fears regarding our home.

Driving during thunderstorms became more stressful. I'll never forget driving him to school during a horrendous storm. I could see the clouds ahead and that the sky was breaking. I knew that after a few miles, the worst would be over. But until that happened, it was awful. He was screaming and terrified like never before. He was afraid we would be stranded in the high water and die in the process. He begged me to turn around and go home and since we were just a few blocks away, I could have easily done this.

It wasn't that I was trying to cause Jason undue stress; but I knew that within 10 minutes we would be on the other side of the storm. The school would have understood completely if Jason missed the day. Many kids at the school had their share of anxieties and they were used to this. It was a constant struggle between my fear of causing him to have a breakdown and pushing the envelope so that he would realize he would be okay.

As we continued on our route, the rain began to dissipate. He made it safely to school, but I know it was exhausting for him. It wasn't easy for me either. It was plenty for me to have to deal with concentrating on the road and avoiding high water; to have my child screaming in the back seat made it more taxing. But like every other time this happened, we survived. He would constantly watch The Weather Channel and watch their show, "Storm Stories". In my opinion, this only fueled his anxiety even more but for whatever reason, he had to know about storms and what causes them. In his case, maybe the knowledge about our climate offered some comfort. Now in his teenage years,

Jason has outgrown his fears of inclement weather. He continues to be interested in the sciences and I think that part of him always will be.

Ryan's fear of the weather was worse than Jason's ever was. If Jason was inside our home, he felt safe to a reasonable degree. Yes, he would fixate on The Weather Channel and be concerned about floods. But with Ryan, he completely isolated himself. The way his room was set up, he faced a window when he watched television. He could see the lightning come through the shade and this caused more anxiety. He would move to my bedroom where the window was behind him while he was watching his shows.

All of the lights had to be on, regardless of it being day or night. When lightning struck and shined through, he was terrified. There were several months where my schedule was on hold. I could make plans but was never sure if I could keep them. I couldn't leave him because he was SO scared. One of our lowest periods was when he would go inside my walk-in closet with his pillow and blanket and lay on my floor. Keep in mind that my closet was not that big but Ryan seemed to manage. He would play his games or read a book so that he wouldn't have to see any lightning come through the window.

My heart broke for him. Had my closet been big enough, I would have sat with him and tried to comfort him. Occasionally, I could convince him to lie on my bed with me so we could watch his shows together. He would wear a baseball cap so it would block some of the reflection of the storms. Other times he would wrap a towel or blanket around his head, only allowing his eyes to peak through. But then his head would get overheated being wrapped up for so long. It was a better alternative than him being frightened; I just felt so badly for him that he was so scared.

Today, he is somewhat better. If it is raining out, I can usually leave him and he only occasionally goes inside my closet. He continues to be obsessed with the weather and checking the forecast, though. If it even looks like it's going to rain or if rain is predicted within three days, he begins perseverating on it. However, I am very thankful that it is more manageable than in years past.

As parents, we teach our kids to follow the rules and tell the truth. Kids like mine take this to the extreme. We bend the rules sometimes and when this occurs, they don't understand. For example, movie prices increase when your child reaches a certain age. At our theatre, it was when your child turned 12 years old. When Jason turned 13, I still ordered a child ticket because I didn't want to pay the higher price. Both kids thought this was wrong and asked me how I could do such a thing. How could I break the rules? Technically, they were correct. I felt terrible setting a poor example for them. I explained that this was my decision to make and hoped that one day when they were older, they would understand.

The same problem occurred when we went to an amusement park. Ryan had just turned 13 and I told them he was 12 years old. This time, he yelled out to the person behind the ticket counter "I'm not 12! I'm 13 now!" I quickly rebounded and told the man he just turned 13 and it was my mistake. Yes, I had to pay another $8.00. There was no getting out of that one.

These examples might seem trivial to you. I think that most of us try to slide by in situations like this to save a few dollars. To my kids, I was almost a criminal. These kinds of issues came up daily. We had problems when ordering at a restaurant and the kids menu said "Children 10 and under". If my kid was 11 and not a big eater, a kid's portion was just fine for him. Explaining this to them was not an easy task. They think in terms of black and white. You follow the rules and obey laws. People who don't can get arrested and sent to jail. It was and still is for Ryan a part of life that will always need explaining. It took a long time for them to differentiate that breaking a rule does not mean you'll go to jail.

The middle schools they attended had dress codes. Pants had to be khaki or blue with a collared shirt in white or navy. You could wear blue jeans which were a saving grace, easy to maintain and they never wore out. Jackets had to be navy or you could wear sweatshirts purchased at the school store. During colder months, you could wear an undershirt or long sleeved shirt under your collared shirt.

Not Ryan. This was for two reasons. First, you're not supposed to wear two shirts. You should wear only one shirt. Second, the undershirt didn't have a collar and went against school policy. I explained the "exception" to the rule and even showed him the school website. It didn't help. So he carries a jacket with him wherever he goes. We have lightweight navy jackets, medium weight navy jackets, and heavy weight navy jackets. One time, we couldn't find his lightweight jacket and I tried to get him to take another one that was navy but had a very tiny stripe down the side. Not a chance! He wouldn't even consider taking it because of the stripe. He ended up taking the heavier jacket instead. I explained it would be fine and I would even e-mail the school but that wasn't good enough for Ryan.

Closing doors – is this a rule or a ritual? Ryan is always closing doors as part of his lifestyle, so at times it's more of a ritual. It's not a rule when you're just watching television in your room and you want the door closed. But when he is sleeping, the door must be closed. Normally this isn't a problem but there was a short period when it was. Living in an older home in Houston, the house sometimes shifts and resettles. As a result, the door hits the frame and won't close. This drove Ryan absolutely crazy. After a couple of weeks, it would usually readjust itself but not the last time. The door was ajar and he couldn't handle it. It would take him forever to fall asleep because he knew the door wasn't closed all the way. Like his other extreme rituals, he perseverated endlessly on it. When it was obvious it wasn't going to resettle on its own, I had the door shaved so it could close again. You have never seen such a happy child when he came home from school and the door was fixed. If he's happy, I'm happy.

When I'm in the bathroom and putting on makeup or drying my hair, the door is open. If I'm just brushing my teeth or combing my hair, the door is still open. Not Ryan – he closes the door for everything. It doesn't matter what he's doing, the door is always closed. It may not seem like a big deal, but it is when you want to put something away in the bathroom or someone else needs to use it. The boys share a bathroom, and Ryan can take a long time in there. He sometimes starts pacing back and forth and flapping his hands and can be in there for 20 minutes when he should be out much quicker. I've explained that the door can be open sometimes, but Ryan disagrees. I just let him do his thing because there are other issues that are much more important.

During 4th and 5th grades, Jason joined the safety patrol at school. I was very proud of him as this was a daily commitment to be at his post no later than 7:30am. School didn't begin until 8:00am and it was wonderful that he wanted to help the supervising teacher make sure that all the kids arrived safely. I always made sure he arrived on time and was respectful of the 7:30 rule.

One night, Jason had a terrible time falling asleep. I can't remember what the obsession of the day was at that moment in time, but he was worried about something. When it came time to wake him up the next day, I woke him up later than usual. Typically, I woke him up at 6:30 but on that day, I got him up at 7:15. I told him I would take him to school at 7:45 in plenty of time for the 8:00 bell. Unless you saw it for yourself, it would be incomprehensible for you to understand how he reacted. He became unglued – completely hysterical. He was terrified because students are to report no later than 7:30 for safety patrol. If you were late, you received a demerit. Jason would equate this with a death sentence.

He said "Mom, you don't understand the rules! You have to follow the rules. You can't change the rules. There are no exceptions!" He repeated this over and over again and was inconsolable. He was falling apart before my eyes. I immediately called the Safety Patrol teacher and explained what happened. As you would imagine, she completely agreed with me that extra sleep was more important. I had her speak with Jason and he finally calmed down. He was still upset with me but was very relieved the teacher was not upset and that he didn't receive a demerit.

Every teacher absolutely loves my kids. They are always respectful, polite, and want to help whenever they're asked. This didn't always sit well with their peers, especially in middle school. We all remember those years; they were really rough. No longer in elementary school yet not in high school and those hormones are starting to kick in. I've always praised my kids for being model students and following the rules. Problems begin when their peers don't feel the way they do.

In 8th grade, Jason went to one of his classes as usual. The teacher wasn't there and there was no substitute teacher. The students were thrilled to be left alone. At first, they were just having fun. Some of the kids became very loud and wild. Jason was nervous because he knew that the school policy was that students were not to be left alone. A teacher was to be in the class at all times. He told some of the other kids it wasn't a good idea to be in the class unsupervised. They didn't care what he thought and were happy to have a free period. When he told them he was going to the front office to let them know, the other kids became angry. They told him not to go and he explained again that something bad could happen. He left the class and reported that there was no teacher in their class.

He was told by the front office that his teacher was absent. There was a mix-up as to what time the substitute teacher was to arrive and the school secretary really appreciated Jason letting her know. When Jason came home from school that day, he had mixed emotions. He knew he did the right thing by going to the front office but was upset the kids were so angry at him. He has such a conscience and would have felt terrible if a student had gotten hurt while being unsupervised. This is one of those moments as a parent when you know your child did the right thing but feel terrible that they're ostracized in the process. I did my best to reassure him that he did the right thing.

Both kids have been mainstreamed since middle school; they often utilized resource teachers and benefited from the smaller classes or one on one time to help them grasp different subjects. The policy was for students to show up for their regular class, check in with the teacher and then report to the resource teacher. Normally, this policy worked well. The mainstream teachers knew how my kids followed the rules and the resource teachers knew when to expect them. One day, Jason went to his regular class but the teacher wasn't there. There was a substitute teacher. Other kids were acting up and the teacher was frustrated. When Jason approached him to check in, the teacher told him to sit down. He didn't want to discuss anything and wanted the class to settle down. This completely threw Jason off because he knew he had to get to his resource class. He waited a couple of minutes but the teacher still wasn't interested in what he had to tell him. This caused more anxiety and he became upset. His eyes started to tear up and the teacher finally noticed something wasn't right. He realized what Jason was trying to tell him and allowed him to leave the class.

Times like this are hard for my kids because they are following the rules but are reprimanded because of the other kids. They do not understand why teachers penalize the entire class because of the actions of a few. My kids would never do anything to jeopardize a relationship with a teacher or other person of authority. It's extremely difficult for them to comprehend why they have to miss out on something when they did nothing wrong and followed the rules. When they asked me why this happens, there are times I don't have a reason to give them. I would explain that the teacher made this decision and while neither of us agreed with it, we had to respect them for it.

It's stressful for any student to make sure they have the right books for the right class at all times. Changing classes can also be nerve-wracking because the halls are crowded and noisy. Due to his fear of possibly being late to the next class, Jason would focus more on the time than the material being taught. He was okay during 75% of the class. But when he knew it was the end of the class period, he would keep looking at the clock and mentally getting himself and his books ready for the next class. Teachers began to notice he looked agitated and asked why. He explained he wanted to make sure he was on time for his next class. The assistant principal was very understanding and allowed him to leave class 5 minutes early so he wouldn't worry. I can promise you he wasn't learning anything anyway since he was so distracted by his anxiety, so at that point he was better off heading to the next class.

When Ryan turned 13, I began leaving him alone for short periods of time to run quick errands. He was very excited and it reminded him of the boy in the movie "Home Alone". This was a major step for me because I hadn't left him alone before. I felt he would be okay but had to explain the rules every time I left. There were rules about when he should answer the telephone and what to say. Caller ID was one of the best inventions because it would let him know who was calling. I always reminded him that if he did not recognize the name, he should not pick up the phone. There were rules if someone rang the doorbell and who was allowed in. I always had a list of emergency phone numbers and called frequently while I was out. Many kids are babysitting by his age and I was just happy that I could leave him for short spells and not have to take him with me. He much preferred being at home. All of these rules are typical when you leave your kids home alone.

Ryan is now 15 and I am still repeating the same rules. Yes, I can leave him for longer periods and this is great progress. But for typically developing kids, they get it after awhile. Kids like Ryan have to have rules drilled into them over and over. I never take anything for granted and assume that he will remember what to do. If anything ever happened because I wasn't home, I would be devastated and never forgive myself. I know that it is part of letting go and making sure you've covered your bases as best you can. I guess this is the fear within me that I have to cope with every day. In this way, I can relate to my kids only too well.

Please, stop picking on my child!

Years ago when my kids were diagnosed with autism, I remember coming across a series of informational tapes to help guide parents to help their kids interact with their peers. At the time, Jason was in elementary school and Ryan was in preschool. The tapes discussed how to help your child cope with their difficulty in making friends and help them deal with being picked on. I listened intently and took mental notes as to what to be on the lookout for and for the best way to help my kids. Little did I know at the time just how prophetic the tapes would be and that they were a precursor of what was to come in the years ahead.

The expert on the subject was a practicing psychologist on the east coast with vast experience working with special needs kids and their social skills. I was immediately taken with these tapes and all they had to offer. At the time, I prayed that my kids might be different and not encounter these problems. There was that hope that, just maybe, my kids would be spared some of these hurts.

You have no idea how I wish I could write that this was the case. Sadly, there have been many years where they were the target of bullies or kids who were obnoxious and took great pleasure in annoying them.

I'm the first to tell you that each one of us has to learn how to cope with people who can be mean spirited. Having special needs or not, no one gets a free ride. But kids are not going to leave your child alone because they have special needs. If a child has a physical disability, kids can be very cruel. A friend of mine had a mild case of cerebral palsy and kids would tease her all the time about the way she walked. I think that it's even more confusing when your child has a disability the other kids can't "see". They don't understand why my children bring up topics that have nothing to do with the conversation at hand or why the teacher has to explain subjects differently and in a manner my kids can understand. They look just like other kids yet act differently.

As I mentioned in an earlier chapter, our first experience in coping with bullies was during Jason's kindergarten year. It was truly one of the longest school years we ever had. How I wish these kids would have left Jason alone and that he could have just ignored them, but this wasn't possible. It was a very small school and he had to see these two kids multiple times a day. As a parent, the pain I felt for my child was enormous. I wanted to tell them to leave my child alone and to call their parents and tell them the same thing. Of course I couldn't do this, but in my heart I was dying to do something. After school, Jason would perseverate on what happened during these days and was unable to let it go.

Truthfully, I don't blame him. It is difficult to just let it go when you're the target and being picked on. I explained to him that while I didn't have to deal with kids like this in kindergarten, I had a terrible time in middle school and high school. There was a neighbor kid that was always trying to pick a fight with me when I was 14. She was 15 and lived on my street, which was even worse. I was always afraid of running into her while hanging out with other kids. Her family was really strange and didn't associate much with the other families on the block so it wasn't like my parents could approach hers.

After a year of agony, she finally left me alone. In 10th grade, there was a 9th grade boy who was always annoying me. I had to ride the bus with him and absolutely dreaded seeing him. As he was always being sarcastic and saying mean things, I couldn't wait until the year was over when I would receive my driver's license. I was thrilled to get away from this kid and elated to have the freedom to never have to take the bus again. Those two experiences truly made my teenage years miserable and I completely understand why any child would be upset. I know how it made me feel and I was older than Jason when these things happened to me.

As painful as it was for me, it's worse when it's your child. The worst incident was when one of the kids tied Jason to a pole during recess. It was cruel and humiliating, and caused so much emotional damage. His teacher was not present. Clearly, the other teacher supervising the group was not keeping an eye on the kids. I was devastated that this happened and I felt such tremendous pain for Jason. I couldn't wait until the year was over and hoped Jason didn't encounter extreme kids like that ever again. If he did, I prayed it wasn't until he was much older.

Since this was only kindergarten, concerned does not begin to describe how I felt about the remaining elementary school years. As it turned out, we had our ups and downs. Third grade was nothing spectacular and 5th grade was quite difficult. It just killed me to see Jason treated this way by other kids. As much as I tried to help him cope with it and have these kids reprimanded by their teachers, it was a never ending cycle.

As you would expect, middle school became more complicated. Kids talked back to teachers and were mean to each other on a regular basis. Jason kept to himself for the most part in 6th grade but did become friends with one other boy. They had a few classes together and had the same lunch period which was even better. He was a great kid and they even got together occasionally outside of school. I was thrilled that he clicked with him and they're friends to this day as seniors in high school.

Some of the other kids were not as kind. They were always breaking the rules, which Jason would never dream of doing. He always respected his teachers and was a model student. Kids who were the class clown or rebellious did not like rule followers like Jason. They couldn't relate to Jason any more than Jason could relate to them. It was exhausting explaining to him that some kids are just like this and he should do his best to avoid them. But someone acting this way was too foreign to him, and he didn't understand. In 8th grade, he applied for and was chosen to become a front office worker during his elective period. He chose this over all of the other options and had a great relationship with his assistant principal. She loved having him as her helper, as did the rest of the other administrative staff. He took great pride in helping them with whatever they needed; it was a wonderful experience for him.

The problem was that it did not make him popular with some of the other students. They knew how well liked Jason was by all of his teachers and house principals. I stressed to him that he was an amazing student and should not change for anyone. It's complicated because being a teenager is problematic enough as it is. Kids want to fit in and have friends but they have to do it within the realm of what they're comfortable with. And Jason was content and calm always following the rules. I know there were incidences that he never told me about. He was trying to take care of the difficulties on his own and didn't want his mother intervening. I can respect this, I truly can. Being the ever so caring parent, I still wanted to help him in any way possible.

A few of the kids from middle school went to the same high school and, thankfully, they were the kids that Jason got along with. Overall, high school has been a great experience for Jason. The entire school is very small with not more than 400 kids. He has had his share of friends and they stuck together. I have no doubt there are kids at his school who have been bullied and my heart goes out to these kids. I'm grateful that Jason was not a target. While I imagine there were problems that Jason declined to tell me about, I think that his high school years have been pretty positive.

Ryan's elementary school years went quite well too. There was the occasional kid who would annoy him but overall, he went through the years unscathed.

And then middle school arrived. It has been most taxing. Sixth grade went well. Luckily, he had an aide with him during many of his 6th grade classes. The principal was well aware of Ryan's special needs and his needing extra help. The aide floated from class to class and worked with Ryan and two other students. The comfort of knowing that someone was keeping a close eye on him was immeasurable. I knew that he wouldn't have an aide forever; I was just relieved that he had someone for the majority of his 6th grade year. Toward the end of the year, he even told his aide to walk several steps behind him because he could find his way himself to the next class. All of this was a good thing because it showed that Ryan was becoming independent and maturing. But even though this was a positive step for Ryan, it was scary for me.

The next two years became increasingly trying. In 7th grade, he only met with his aide sporadically and the aide would check on Ryan periodically during his classes. But it was not constant like in 6th grade because the school felt that Ryan had come so far. While I knew I had to let him be on his own during classes, there was always that part of me that wanted him to have someone with him. I was still able to e-mail his aide whenever I needed to if there were questions about assignments or if problems arose between Ryan and another student. But it wasn't the same and I had to keep telling myself that this was part of Ryan growing up.

He often came home with stories of kids bothering him. Ryan was so sensitive and constantly wanted to know why kids acted the way they did. I didn't always have an answer which made matters worse. Telling Ryan that they were just acting out to get attention was not good enough. Explaining to him that they were trying to get a reaction out of him didn't help either. He just wanted them to stop and couldn't get it off of his mind. Kids would steal his pencils, erasers, or purposely knock his notebook on the floor. This drove him crazy.

There was one girl in particular who really knew how to push Ryan's buttons. I knew she wasn't doing anything that terrible; I just hated that she was annoying my child so much. Having the teachers talk to her didn't help much. It was just the way it was. Ryan tended to perseverate even more than Jason did. He could go on for hours about kids that drove him crazy and wouldn't leave him alone. We talked about it constantly and what he could do to handle it. I had a great relationship with his teachers and the administrative staff. I knew that Ryan could misinterpret the actions of others sometimes and I would e-mail the teachers to get the real scoop. The teachers were incredible and always tried. But they had so many students to manage and they could only do so much.

As I write this chapter, Ryan is now in 8th grade. His aide has been scaled back to only helping him with special assignments and projects. He is completely on his own and while I am so proud of him for getting to his classes on his own and completing assignments independently, the social interaction with his classmates has deteriorated. The beginning of the year was tolerable and we only had intermittent moments of dwelling on what happened at school.

As the year progressed, Ryan encountered more problems. Now there is only a month left of school and I couldn't be happier. The last several weeks have been building and this week has been awful. Kids make fun of him because of some of the questions he asks the teacher. Ryan has been in class with these same kids for the 3rd year in a row; they're very tuned into his tics and unusual behaviors, which make him a target. Between the spitballs, kids stealing his pencils, and trying to get money from him, I can't begin to tell you how sad and frustrated I've been. When I ask Ryan where the teachers are, he is the first to tell me these kids are sent to the principal's office, receive detention, or have privileges taken away. I know the teachers are trying their best to keep the kids in line. Given their age and it being the end of the school year, it's quite the battle. As I've wished before when this happened, I would love to give these kids a piece of my mind or call their parents. Since I can't, I e-mail the teachers to get their feedback. They feel terrible that it's happening and try to nip it in the bud. The kids involved have been reprimanded and talked to in hopes they will try to have more understanding for kids like Ryan.

After e-mailing the teachers to let them know how much Ryan was affected by this, I started crying when I read one of the teacher's replies. I could feel how badly she felt that this was happening in her class. She has a few kids that are such troublemakers and it's been a trying year. She will reassign Ryan's seat again in hopes of alleviating some of the problems in her class. I e-mailed her back and thanked her for her help.

Another child constantly tells Ryan during lunch that he owes him money. Ryan knows it isn't true but still asks me all the time if it could be. Each time, I emphasize that he does not owe anyone at the school any money. The only person that receives money is the cafeteria staff and his teachers when he attends field trips. No one else! At that moment, Ryan will say okay as though it has finally sunk in. But it comes right back when these kids pester him again.

One time, he asked me if he should respond with a clever comeback and say "Do you think I was born yesterday? I don't owe you any money!" He then proceeded to tell me that it was just an expression about being born yesterday. I had to keep from smiling because I knew what he was referring to. He thought I had no clue as to what "born yesterday" meant. I told him I knew what he meant and he could respond like that or just ignore the kid. In e-mailing the school, they addressed the problem to make sure this does not happen again.

Ryan has tried to talk to Jason about what goes on at school. Being the older brother and having lived through middle school, Jason told him you don't want to be thought of as a snitch. It only makes it worse and the kids will pick on you even more. It's heartbreaking for me to think that my kids and others don't believe they should reach out to their parents or teachers at times like this. My kids occasionally let me help them but other times, they just sat in silence and suffered. How I wish that my kids and others believed more that parents can help them without making it worse for them. There are ways for the school to address these problems without the bullies knowing where the complaints came from. It was most difficult to convince my kids this was possible.

When I hear the horror stories on the news of kids being bullied to their breaking point, it terrifies me. My kids have never received vicious text messages, had pictures of them posted on the internet, or have been physically attacked. It is frightening what is going on today and how extreme it has become. We had our problems when I was growing up but nothing like what I see today. I'm very grateful their being picked on has not reached that extreme but it has still been distressing to deal with through the years. At times, I wish my kids could walk around with a sign that says "Special Needs – Please Handle with Care!" I know this isn't realistic but when it's your child, you want to protect them at all times. It isn't fair how other kids have treated them. Sadly, no one ever said life was fair.

Honesty, Common Sense, and Being Naive

All of these personality traits are connected. People can be so honest; they can't believe that others are not like they are. If you don't have common sense, you may not even realize it because you don't know any differently. For someone who is naïve, you are so trusting that again, you think others are just like you.

Is honesty always the best policy? For the most part, I think it is. I've raised my kids to be truthful in their words and actions. I've led by example as my parents did for me. But what about those moments when you shouldn't be completely honest because you don't want to hurt someone's feelings? What about those times when some information is just too personal and you don't want to answer a question posed to you? Life is full of these situations and we navigate through them on a daily basis. At a young age, we don't have the knowledge to always know what to say and can be ill at ease in social settings. Through daily experiences, parents, teachers and those wiser than us correct and guide our children as to what are appropriate answers. The hope is that our children retain what they've been taught.

Common sense means having good sense and sound judgment in practical matters. Parents hope their children develop common sense and intuition to guide them through social interactions and life's challenges. What if your child hasn't developed that common sense yet? What if that intuitive behavior hasn't surfaced to the top? Jason has developed more common sense through the years and I pray Ryan does as well. Just the other day, Ryan told me he left his jacket in my car and he needed it for school. I told him to get his shoes on and I'd get the jacket. He then asked me, "How will you know which one it is?" I told him that he's been wearing the same jacket for the last 5 months; I'll know which one to get. It wasn't even an issue for me, but Ryan didn't have the wherewithal to know this.

He recently had to attend Saturday tutorials. As a treat, I told him he could pick the place where we could have lunch. He said he wasn't sure where he wanted to go. I told him to think about it and he could let me know when I picked him up. He was confused by what I had said and asked me, "For a few hours?" I quickly realized what he was asking me. He wanted to know if he should think about where he wants to eat for the next three hours while he's in tutorials. I told him to just think about it during break time and to try and concentrate on the material being taught. It never ceases to amaze me how literal he is and how little common sense he has. Once in awhile, he'll surprise me and figure out something on his own. But more often than not, he needs further explanation.

Naïve means having or showing a lack of experience, judgment or information. People on the autism spectrum can sometimes lack common sense and be very naïve which makes them a target during childhood and beyond.

If a child is socially awkward, deficient in the common sense department or naïve, it's understandable because they are children and still learning. But I know autistic adults who come across as very rude in how they respond in social situations and it can be quite shocking. We all have friends who have no common sense or are gullible. I tend to be compassionate and more cognizant of adults with special needs because of my own kids.

Many people are not as understanding of adults like this and believe the person is just being impolite and offensive. If an adult lacks common sense, we often think they're not the sharpest tool in the shed and may not respect their opinion as much. I've said before that when kids do this, we accept it more readily. As they grow up, we expect more of them. This adds to the pressure of parents like me because I sometimes feel the need to explain why my child spoke or acted inappropriately. The concern of how they will be as adults is even more worrisome.

My kids are so honest, at times to a fault. One day I wasn't feeling well and had an upset stomach. I was a few minutes late in getting Jason to elementary school. He was ready to tell the other kids and teacher, "My mom was late and had to keep going to the bathroom." I explained that while this is true, this is too much information and way too personal. A more appropriate explanation would be, "My mom isn't feeling well and that's why I am late."

I learned early on that it was not a good idea for my kids to open gifts in front of guests. It's not that Jason or Ryan would intentionally hurt someone's feelings. But it took only one time for Jason to open a gift and say, "I don't like playing with these," for me to decide that opening gifts should happen at home. There is that lack of impulse control combined with honesty and I couldn't take the chance of them blurting out their true thoughts again. From then on, we brought the gifts home and opened them privately.

Fortunately, in recent years, friends and family will ask me what to get them and this makes life a lot easier. I do the same with my friends. Years ago, we would buy gifts. Now, we buy gift cards or give cash. Kids today are usually saving up for some big ticket item or they're into electronics. Target, Game Stop, or Best Buy gift cards are a sure hit with my kids.

On Ryan's 15th birthday, he received a card from a close family member. I thought it was okay for him to open it because if anything was said that shouldn't have been, she would understand. He opened up the card and inside was a gift card to Marble Slab Creamery. The problem is Ryan doesn't eat ice cream. He did when he was 4 or 5 years old and then just stopped for no reason. A couple of years ago, Ryan would have immediately opened the card and said, "I don't like ice cream." This time, he paused for a second and just said thank you. I was SO proud of him.

As soon as we got home, I sat him down and told him how wonderful it was that he didn't tell the person who gave him the gift that he doesn't like ice cream. I stressed how polite he was and that he did the right thing by just saying thank you for the gift. This may not seem like a big deal to most parents when your child is 15 years old. This was a huge step for Ryan and for me as a parent. So much has to be repeated over and over again with both kids and while the information may appear to sink in, all can be forgotten when they are "in the moment".

Coupled with their honesty is a naïve quality that is

within. This naïveté makes it very difficult to prepare them for life's encounters. How can you teach and anticipate every experience or dilemma to come their way? It's impossible because no one can predict the future. It takes a tremendous amount of coaching and always being not just one step ahead, but multiple steps ahead. Is this exhausting at times? Absolutely. Does it get easier each year? Yes and no. Some information finally gets across and they're able to interact more in accordance with their ages. On the other hand, they are now 19 and 16 and more is expected of them. We're always playing that game of catch-up and continue to have our moments.

Before my mom moved to Houston, she would visit us throughout the year. In between visits, we would call each other almost every day. She has a wonderful relationship with my kids and is a very loving grandmother. She always wanted to talk to her grandchildren and when they were younger, they eagerly came to the phone. As they hit the teenage years, they got caught up in their homework, games, and television shows. She would frequently ask Ryan, "Do you miss me?" Ryan would sometimes reply, "Not sure." He is so honest. He loves his grandma in his own way but he lives in the moment, and if he isn't thinking about her that very minute, he doesn't miss her. When their conversations were finished, she always ended with, "I love you." In true Ryan form, he replied with either, "Okay" or "I know." Occasionally, he would say, "I love you, too." I just never knew what response she would get. She knew him well enough that her feelings weren't hurt. That's just Ryan and he is who he is.

I've tried to train the kids to rinse their dishes and put them in the dishwasher. I continue to remind them to put their clothes in the hamper and keep their rooms neat. Ryan's room can be messy but is tolerable. Jason's room is a disaster. Half the time you can't see the floor. There is a small area that's cleared from the door to his bed. Putting clothes in his closet is quite the challenge because you have to go through that obstacle course to reach the closet. Clearly, they both have much to improve on in the housekeeping department. In this respect, they are typical teenagers.

Now that my mom lives nearby, she watches the kids for me when I'm out of town on business. A few months ago, my mom came over to spend the night. Ryan was in my room watching one of his shows. She went in his room first and there were clothes lying on the floor and a plate on the table. When she found him in my room, there was another plate and a cup on the table. She told him, "Ryan, I'm not happy right now. You've left clothes on the floor and dishes in your room and your mom's room. You need to take care of cleaning this up."

Ryan replied, "Is this the part where I say okay?"

My mom said, "Well only if you mean it!" I guess he didn't mean it because he continued to watch his show. Shortly thereafter, he got up to clean. When she told me the story, I cracked up. As I'm typing this, I'm laughing because it is too funny. He was being so honest in his reply and you really do have to laugh at that kind of thing.

Another time, Ryan was playing one of his Wii games with my adult nephew. He knows how much Ryan loves his games. He asked him, "Ryan, if I gave you $1000, could I have your Wii?"

Ryan said, "No."

He followed up with, "What if I gave you $10,000, would you give me your Wii?" Again, the answer was no.

"Ryan, what if I gave you a million dollars?" The answer was still, "No."

My nephew then asked "Would you give me your Wii for 10 million dollars?" As expected, Ryan said no. My nephew told him that with 10 million dollars, he could buy so many Wii systems. He asked "Ryan, why won't you give me your Wii?"

Ryan's answer? "Because my games are saved on it."

Ryan could easily play all of the games on another system and they'd be saved in no time. There was zero concept of having all of this money to give up his existing Wii. He thinks in such concrete terms and only about what is important to him at the time. You and I know that my nephew was talking in extremes and there was never any money. But Ryan didn't know that. He really thought that he could receive millions of dollars. This didn't matter to him because he was only thinking about his saved games.

Food has always been an issue with both kids. I realize this isn't unusual and while I've seen kids who eat everything under the sun, many are limited to chicken tenders, pizza, hamburgers, hot dogs, and pasta. Fruits and vegetables are not at the top of the list and French fries are not considered a vegetable. When they were babies, I gave them all the right baby foods and snacks that were healthy. It was not an issue and probably the healthiest eating regimen of their lives. Everything started to change with both kids when they were toddlers. For Jason, this happened when he was around four years old and for Ryan, when he was around two and a half years old. They would eat certain foods and then just stop. No warning, no reason – it just ended. They're very sensitive to smells and if they didn't like the way it smelled, there was no chance they would eat it.

In addition, Ryan was tactile defensive from an early age. To some of you reading this, it may sound ridiculous. It was actually our occupational therapist who concluded this after her evaluation. Ryan would not eat foods because of the way they felt. He preferred hard, crunchy foods and not soft ones. I'd have to buy dried fruits and vegetables because the texture was more appealing to him. He has improved but we still have a long way to go.

So why am I bringing up their eating habits? When we were invited to friends' houses when they were younger, this created problems. The hostess would often ask, "Is everything okay?" My kids would be honest and say, "I don't like this," or, "This is terrible." Again, they weren't trying to be rude or impolite. They just replied honestly. They were asked a question and gave you an honest answer.

In order to avoid these awkward moments, I would have many social gatherings in my home. I didn't have to worry what was served or what my kids would say. Was hosting gatherings at my house an extreme reaction to this? I don't believe it was. We could go to the homes of my close friends because they understood how my kids were and weren't offended if I brought food for them to eat. But not everyone feels this way. I know people who believe that children should eat what is put in front of them. Unless there was an allergy, they should eat what everyone else is eating. I never had the chance to think like this because my kids were, and still are, so sensitive to how foods look and smell. I've been told that I'm spoiling my kids and making excuses for them. That's fine; people can think that. I know differently and what makes my kids tick. While I wish they were a bit more adventurous eaters, I have a lot more important things to worry about.

While most kids get their driver's license at 16, Jason waited until he was 17. I believe it was best for him and having that extra year to mature made a huge difference. I'm no different than any other parent when it comes to my child driving. I have the same worries about him being careful and concerns about that first car accident, which was inevitable. All new drivers have to be educated at some point about insurance and what to do if you're in accident. My boyfriend and I explained this to Jason so many times so he would be an informed driver.

The day came when he was on his way to school one morning. Not more than a mile from our house; he rear ended the car in front of him. I was out of town on business which was very frustrating because I would have driven right over. He called me from his cell phone and I could hear him telling the other driver, "Don't worry, sir. This is 100% my fault and I'll pay for all of the damages." I immediately told Jason to NOT say that again. Even though I knew it was his fault, I didn't want to pay for damages that had nothing to do with him hitting the car. Jason was ready to call the police. I explained this was unnecessary and that I wanted to talk to the other driver to get a feel for the situation. At first, Jason was very angry and said I was breaking the law. He argued with me about calling the police and that this must be done.

It was exasperating talking to him and I kept telling him to put the other driver on the phone. I wanted to get a feel for what the other driver was thinking. If the damages were minor and I could pay out of my own pocket, this was my first choice. Filing with our insurance company would guarantee our rates would skyrocket but explaining this to Jason was a lost cause. He kept emphasizing the need to call the police and that this was the law. I finally convinced him to let me talk to the other driver.

The gentleman was very nice and I made sure he was okay. There were no injuries and the damage to his car was minor. I asked him to provide his information to Jason and we would do the same. I explained I was out of town and would contact him within a couple of days; the man was fine with this. I then talked to Jason who had calmed down quite a bit. I explained what the other driver and I agreed upon. He was feeling better and went off to school.

As promised, I tried to contact the other driver several times. I never heard back from him and explained this to Jason. The man's car was over 10 years old and his insurance company was a name I had never heard of. The address he provided was invalid and I was unable to locate him on the internet. In explaining this to Jason, I told him it's more than likely that the man never even had insurance. Furthermore, he was probably a transient who did not want to pursue further contact with us.

I had a strange feeling when I talked to the man the day of the accident because he was very hesitant to give me any information. To try and explain this to Jason was next to impossible the day of the accident. He just thought I was trying to evade the laws and believed I was being dishonest. When it turned out I was correct in my thoughts about this man, he realized I knew more about the situation than he did.

A few months later, Jason rear-ended another driver. Again, I was out of town. It was beyond frustrating for me that this happened again and I could not drive right over to help. When Jason called me, he was so scared because there was serious damage to his front end. The other driver was okay and so was Jason. I stressed to him that a car is only a car. He was the most important part of all of this and I just wanted him to be okay. Everything else can be fixed. Like any kid, he was nervous to call me because this was the second time he caused an accident. I remained calm and was grateful he was not hurt.

I heard him telling the other driver, "Don't worry sir, this is my fault and I'll pay for all of the damages." I immediately told Jason, "Please don't say that again — it's bad enough you said it the first time." I was also thinking, didn't we have this conversation a few months ago? In the moment, we all can forget what we've learned and Jason was and still is a classic case at times like this. I know he was being honest as usual and wanted to do the right thing. It was maddening that I couldn't see the damage for myself because when he told me there was a lot of damage to his car, I didn't know what that meant. A dented hood could be serious damage in Jason's eyes. I felt so badly for him because he was so upset. I wanted to talk to the other driver but needed to calm him down first. I was hoping that he could exchange insurance information again and I could take care of it without filing a claim. As it turns out, the accident was more serious and a passerby had called the police. I had to end my conversation with Jason so the police could investigate the accident.

Once the officer gathered the needed information, I was able to talk to her and the tow truck driver. Jason's car was not in driving condition and had to be towed to the city lot. I called my mom and by the time she got there, everything was about wrapped up. She, too, could see he was upset and tried to reassure him that the most important thing was that he was okay. She talked to the officer who told her that Jason was so polite and such a nice young man.

Yes – that's Jason and I am very proud of him! The problem is his honesty and automatically admitting fault. The next time he has an accident, it could be a gray area as to who is to blame. I'm trying to teach Jason that while you always take responsibility for your mistakes, you have to be careful because there are people who will take advantage of his honesty. We all survived the experience and $3000 later, his car was fixed. This is one of the main reasons I bought him a very used car; I had a feeling there would be times like this.

On a much lighter note, Ryan went to the market with me recently. As I parked the car, he proceeded to tell me I wasn't within the lines of the parking space. I was slightly over the one of the lines but it was fine because it was an area for the shopping carts and was not another parking space. Not for Ryan. He would not get out of the car until I backed up and straightened it out. He was afraid that if I parked over the line that the police would take us to jail. I think some kid at school told him this and of course, he believed them. I told him that while you want to stay within the lines of a parking spot to be courteous to the other drivers; you cannot be arrested if you don't. I would hope that a typical 15-year-old would know this. For Ryan, there is always some clarifying to do since he is not your average kid.

Middle school was very confusing for Ryan and I had to do a lot of explaining during these years. He often came home with farfetched stories that other kids told him and he believed to be true. He had fears of having to repeat grades or go to summer school because other kids had convinced him of this. I had many discussions with him that he would not fail a grade, receive detention, or attend summer school.

Kids can be mean and some of them loved antagonizing Ryan for their amusement. They made up stories because they knew he was gullible. Some of these kids had major behavior issues and in their case, detention was a regular occurrence and summer school was definitely happening for them. I can't tell you the number of times I had to reassure Ryan that he would not fail a grade. Toward the end of each school year, he brings up the topic even more because that's when schools decide who passes onto the next level or who is a candidate for summer school. In a very delicate way, I explained that his teachers would never give him a failing grade. They knew how hard he tried and that he always performed to the best of his ability. This was the explanation given to Ryan in terms he could understand.

As discussed in the previous chapter about both kids acting as the rule police, it is this honesty about them that is their impetus to always follow the rules. Something is either black or white; there is no gray in their minds. While I don't believe rules were made to be broken, I do know that some rules can be bent a bit.

Try to explain this to Jason and Ryan and it's as though I'm speaking in Latin. They often don't understand. I'm able to get through occasionally because they realize that just maybe I know more than they do. Common sense is something you're either born with or you're not. You can't teach it out of a book. Some people are born naïve and that's just their personality. It's scary as a parent because my kids are so sweet and would never take advantage of anyone. It's also very sad because I know they get confused and hurt, and I wish I could always be there to save them. I know this isn't possible and continue to pray that with each year that they will learn a little more and be taken advantage of a lot less.

Thank You for Being a Friend!

For those of you old enough to remember, there was a fabulous show that debuted in 1985 called "The Golden Girls". It was about four women who were previously married and now living together. It was a delightful show that ran for 7 years and I loved watching it. Once in awhile, I even watch the reruns. When I'm their age, I want to live life like these women did. They had their share of problems but they always stayed close and could rely on each other in good times and bad.

The theme song to the show was an abbreviated version of a great song "Thank You for Being a Friend". There is a line in the song, "Your heart is true, you're a pal and a confidante".

This illustrates Jason to a tee. He is a very caring and loyal friend. It wasn't until he got into high school that he truly blossomed and came into his own, having quite a few friends. Jason is a pleaser, and while he sometimes has been able to keep his emotions in check, there have been times when I really had to reel him in. I have explained to him often that he and I are a lot alike and as much as he wants to be a friend, he can't let his friends bring him down completely.

Jason's heart is so true, and he being a confidant to his

friends has at times become extreme. So what's the problem? It affects him so deeply that it permeates into the rest of his life. He believes he has everything under control, and while I respect his opinion, I disagree. I've been there for many friends through very difficult times and they've been there for me. The difference is that I don't let it seep into other parts of my life. He has become exhausted on several occasions, spending so much time trying to help friends out with their crises.

When Jason was younger, it was very hard to explain what a true friend was and how they should behave. There were kids that he considered his friends; you and I would categorize them as acquaintances. In 5th grade, Jason came home one day to tell me that he had a bet with one of the leaders in his safety patrol. Jason was rooting for the Patriots; his friend was for the Rams. The bet was that if the Patriots won, Jason would be excused from safety patrol for one afternoon. If the Rams won, Jason had to work every day for two months. I'm thinking – one day if he wins, two months if he loses. This was not an even bet and if this kid was considered to be his friend, he was not a nice one. I explained to Jason that I doubted the safety patrol teacher would want him betting. Even if she did, this was not a fair bet.

But to Jason, it was okay because he liked safety patrol. Moreover, he really liked the kid who he made the bet with. He trusted him. I had the teacher talk to him and explain that betting is not allowed. Jason became scared and asked if this was a warning to him. He is afraid of warnings and did not want to be kicked off safety patrol. She explained that he did nothing wrong and it was a good thing he told her what the other boy was trying to do. I reassured him as well that he did nothing wrong. It was important for me to make sure that during moments like this, I taught Jason what was the right way to be treated by any friend.

Another time during elementary school, he came home to tell me we need to buy a present for a "friend" at school. I asked Jason if he was invited to the boy's birthday party. I told him that if this child was a good friend and he wasn't having a party, I'd be happy to buy him a present anyway. But to just buy a present for a child he hardly knew, this was not something the boy should have asked him to do. He told Jason he really wanted a new packet of trading cards and he thought Jason would get them for him. Jason wanted to please him and after explaining numerous times why we weren't going to get the present for him, I think he finally understood.

During middle school, Jason had a few friends. There was the boy I mentioned in a previous chapter plus a few other kids who attended different schools. They made plans to see each other, but it was a bit hard because those kids had their own friends at school.

High school came and the sky opened up. It started off slow in 9th grade and with each year came more friends. By Jason's junior year, he became very involved in a community wide youth group and in theatre at his school. These activities had a profound effect on him; they were the two loves of his life and he will cherish the memories with the friends he made. He grew so much being involved with these kids and expanded his horizons. He held board positions in his youth group and had lead roles in school plays. Very much the shining star, he was dedicated and the teachers and youth group advisor loved working with him.

Jason has great friends now, most of them younger than

him. This is fine with me; I just want him to be happy. His friends really look up to him since he is a senior, and he is always there to lend advice. I know they will miss him terribly next year when he is off at college. While they can always keep in touch with Facebook and texting, it isn't the same as being there in person.

Ryan has had a more difficult time with social skills and making friends. I believe that, at times, he wants to have friends and tries to reach out. Yet there are so many times when he doesn't want to go out and is happy to just stay home. Like most kids with autism, his social skills are most awkward and his peers have difficulty relating to him. Middle school has been challenging and I am very sad to write that in three years being at his school, he had one friend over a few times when he was in 6th grade. They seemed to get along well and I thought Ryan enjoyed his company. I don't know why things changed; Ryan never expressed that there were any problems. He just didn't want to get together with this child anymore. He said the boy was nice but he just wasn't interested anymore in making plans with him. I always asked Ryan if there was anyone he wanted to come over or join us at the movies. The answer has always been no.

It makes me sad because I believe Ryan wants his social life to be different. I've recently become friendly with a wonderful lady who is a friend of my boyfriend. She has a 14-year-old son and 12-year-old daughter. Her daughter has become close with my boyfriend's daughter.

Her son was recently diagnosed with a form of autism and I suggested to her that our kids get together. I've gotten to know him and he's a nice kid. She jumped at the chance and I can't tell you how excited I am that the boys are getting together for the first time this weekend. This boy's favorite shows are Family Guy, South Park, and Three Stooges. He loves to play video games and this is Ryan's world to a tee. I feel as though I've won the lottery. She lives about 30 minutes away but even if she lived an hour away, I'd still find a way for the boys to get together. I really feel they will click and I pray Ryan and he get along. I want so much for him to have a new friend that he feels safe with and believe in my heart that this will work.

Ryan eats breakfast and lunch at school. I always make sure to introduce myself to the kitchen staff so they know about Ryan's special needs. He tends to go overboard on what he can have and I make sure they know he can't buy anything and everything. It's all about choices and Ryan has to make his.

In 2009 while Ryan was in the 7th grade, our school district automated the payment system which has been great. I don't have to worry about sending money with Ryan; I can now pay online and it tells me when his account is low. When the system generated an e-mail telling me his account was low one day, I thought it seemed too soon but didn't think much of it and put more money into his account. Then a few weeks later, I receive another e-mail.

This time, I knew there was no way he could have gone through all of the money in such a short time. I met with the kitchen staff; they've always been so kind to me and Ryan. I told them I was concerned because of him going through so much money in such a short amount of time. I know kids go through growth spurts and eat more as a result, but this was not the case. I also talked to the lunch monitor and had them keep an eye on Ryan as well. Sure enough, within a couple of days, they called me. Kids were approaching

Ryan and asking him to buy them breakfast and lunch. The irony is that Ryan doesn't even pay for breakfast – kids eat free. He was eating his breakfast and then paying for a 2nd breakfast for another student. At lunch time, he would eat his lunch and then buy lunch for another student. I didn't blame the school at all that this was happening. School cafeterias are very hectic and it's impossible to keep track of who comes through the food service line.

I knew that I had to confront Ryan in a very gentle way. I needed to find out who was doing it so I could have it stopped. When he told me what was going on, I can't say I was surprised. These kids who would say they were his friends would ask him to help them out. I explained that while I never want a child to go hungry, we don't have the money to buy breakfast and lunch for these kids. I explained that being a single parent, the extra money was not there. Even if it was, I told Ryan in very basic terms that this was not something that could continue.

I stressed that he did nothing wrong and I know he was trying to be a nice friend. But if these other kids were really his friends, they'd understand why he can't buy them food anymore. The teachers also talked to these kids to make sure it didn't happen again. I told Ryan he doesn't have to be mean in telling his friends no. He just had to tell them he can't do it any longer.

As you would expect, the kids told Ryan, "You're not being a good friend." I told Ryan that this wasn't true; he was a very good friend. These kids were asking him to do something that was not his responsibility. Ryan was asked a couple more times when the teachers weren't looking and when he said no, they finally left him alone. I imagine they found another student to target.

It's hard because I explain to Ryan the importance of charity and helping out those who are less fortunate. I donate all old clothes, books, toys and cell phones. Regardless of me being a single parent and on a budget, I will always find a way to help others. It may not be much but it's something. It was hard to explain to Ryan that buying other kids breakfast or lunch was not the same thing. I think he finally understood but again, I always wonder.

As I mentioned earlier, Jason has a heart of gold. He's always giving the other kids rides and that's okay with me. Before Jason could drive, his older friends did the same for him. I occasionally paid them gas money and felt this was the right thing to do. These kids were doing me a huge favor by transporting Jason to various activities. The problem is that Jason is always giving these kids rides and rarely does someone offer to help him pay for gas. Jason will tell you that it's fine and he enjoys doing it. His words are spoken like a true pleaser. To me, it's extreme because it's constant and he'll pick up kids 30 minutes away. All of this adds up and he spends a lot of my money on gas.

On the one hand, I am so happy that Jason has friends and the kids he associates with are really good kids. The majority of kids are younger than him; the two kids that are his age do not have their license yet. On the other hand, it's costing a fortune. Do I think he's being taken advantage of? Sometimes I do. I think once in awhile they could help pay for gas or pay for his meal. At this point, he'll be graduating in a month and what's done is done. My suggestions to him to ask the other kids to help out once in awhile were cast aside. I realize I could have been more firm and told him that I'm reducing his allowance to compensate for the money spent on carting his friends around. Jason does not like conflict with his friends and they mean the world to him. So I let it go this last year and rationalized it in my own mind. He doesn't buy expensive clothes or have a girlfriend he's taking out all the time. I figured I would let it slide as I'm thankful he has such nice friends.

All parents must keep the lines of communication open with their children. With my kids, it's even more imperative. They think they know how something should be handled or believe that someone is really their friend.

In reality, they need continued guidance in this area. I'm not blind and know my kids don't tell me everything; they keep plenty to themselves. Even with all of their special needs, they realize there are certain things they don't want to discuss with mom. I guess my kids are just like yours and we do the best we can to make sure they are protected.

Broadening Their Horizons

We all know kids who will try anything once and if it doesn't work out, they move on to something else. Many parents can enroll their kids in almost any class and not give it a second thought. This has always been foreign to me because I've always had to check out an activity in depth before my kids were signed up. While this was time consuming, it was well worth it to ensure a positive experience for them. It was important to find out the ratio of kids to instructor, age of the other kids in the class and if they had to have any knowledge of the activity. Generally, I enrolled them in beginner level programs but even then, many of the other kids were more advanced than mine.

During their preschool and elementary school years, Jason and Ryan were fairly amenable to various activities. It made my life a lot easier because I didn't have to convince them to participate. They went and seemed to enjoy themselves. I wanted them enrolled with typically developing kids but had to be careful in what I chose.

Team sports were not an option. They never signed up for little league, basketball, or any other competitive sport. Some kids on the autism spectrum adapt well to team sports; I just knew that mine would not. They were not and still aren't coordinated in that way. More importantly, I don't believe they had the personality to interact with their teammates. It's not that I believed my kids weren't good enough or that I'm putting them down. I wanted my kids to participate in anything they had the desire to.

They seemed most comfortable playing an individual sport. It can be a lot of pressure playing in team sports and I didn't want to add to their stress level. I applaud the coaches of these teams as they try to instill camaraderie and team spirit regardless of whether the team won or lost. The problem is that some kids are not as forgiving. I knew without a doubt that if one of my kids had cost the team a win, my kids would be devastated. The pressure would be too much and they would dwell on the loss for weeks. Moreover, some parents are out of control during their kids' games. The yelling and intensity of their actions would make Jason and Ryan even more anxious. I didn't want them exposed to that; it just wasn't worth it to me. Individual activities were the way to go for us.

So I found alternative sports for them where they could still interact with other kids and be exposed to new activities. Gymnastics worked well for Jason and Ryan during the early years. They could get their share of exercise and work on their coordination without the strain of having to excel like the other kids. They developed the skills at their own pace, allowing them to learn in their own way. Neither were superstars in the class but exposure to the balance beam, rings and floor exercises was always a plus in my mind.

They were always the oldest kids in the class because it took them longer to develop the skills needed to take them to the next level. At first, this was difficult for me. The other parents didn't know my kids had special needs. Their kids were younger than Jason and Ryan and they wondered why my kids were in the same class with theirs. I knew my kids were immature and pairing them with their peers would have been taxing.

When I look back, these years were a mixture of sadness and relief. I was sad because my kids had disabilities you couldn't see and people always wondered why they were in classes with kids younger than them. At the same time, I was relieved that I had the opportunity to enroll my kids in gymnastics. The program director and instructors were amazing and I will always be grateful for their patience and understanding. I knew my kids required more time and practice to learn new skills but the instructors never complained.

Jason took classes for a few years, and it was wonderful while it lasted. But the gap between him and the other kids widened. Kids that excelled were serious about it as a sport and were invited to join a competitive team. As Jason grew, there were fewer classes offered as an activity. It became uncomfortable for him and I knew I needed to find something else. Ryan was able to continue for another year but wasn't into it as in previous years. It was time to find something else.

Our life with martial arts began! I had heard from friends how wonderful it is for kids and there was a Korean class called Kuk Sool Won in our neighborhood. It was a fantastic program and I enrolled both kids. Jason was about 8 years old and Ryan was 4 ½. Again, we were blessed with devoted and compassionate instructors who believed that every child can learn and excel. It didn't matter how long it took them. My kids' were not as precise as the other students' but this was okay. The instructors knew my kids were giving it their all for what they were capable of doing. They wanted kids to have a positive attitude and try their best. Jason enjoyed the class more than Ryan did. He actually excelled to the brown belt level and worked very hard on his skills and technique. Ryan did well but was not as enthusiastic as Jason was. He received a couple of stripes on his yellow belt and that was enough for him. When Jason was finishing 5th grade and anticipating middle school and the work load ahead, he told me he didn't want to continue because it was too much for him. Taking classes twice a week and periodic tests were stressing him out. How could I argue with that? Who was I to determine what was too much for him? I really wanted them both to continue taking classes, but I could see his anxiety and it wasn't worth it to me to overload him. Ryan could have continued but I could see he wasn't enjoying it as much. So our life with martial arts classes came to an end but the door was always left open if they wanted to return.

I then found out about a great Boy Scout troop. It's not as though Scouts was new to me; I was a Girl Scout in elementary school. I knew of a troop close to our home but had heard that the kids were very mature and some were not the nicest to be around. This can happen with any troop, but I didn't want to expose Jason to that. When I was told of a different troop that might be better for him, I checked it out and immediately loved it. So we entered the world of Boy Scouts although it was very late in life; he was already in 7th grade.

It didn't seem to matter to the scout leaders. They were incredible and worked with Jason at his own pace to earn his badges. They loved having him and he enjoyed the meetings and getting to know the other kids. The periodic weekend campouts were a great opportunity to see new places and try new things.

I won't deny that I loved the break while he was away. I loved having only one child to focus on and devote my attention to. The important part of all this was that he found something that he enjoyed.

Then 9th grade came and the stress of high school began. He started to feel pressured again and believed that the weekly meetings and campouts were too much. He was usually very tired after these weekend excursions and it made the school week harder for him. I was back to asking myself the same questions as I had with martial arts. Who was I to determine if he could handle high school and the commitment to Scouts? I truly wish he'd been able to continue with the troop but the handwriting was on the wall. The Scoutmaster was very understanding and again, the door was left open for Jason to return. I had a feeling we wouldn't be returning because I could see the pressures mounting on him and that school needed to be the primary focus at this point in his life.

Finding extracurricular activities was more challenging with Ryan. Since he is more delayed than Jason was and more close-minded, finding interests that would excite him was tricky. Our Jewish Community Center worked hard to coordinate programs for special needs kids. They began a Top Soccer program where kids could learn basic soccer skills, have games, and even receive awards. The coach was terrific and he had teenage volunteers for each child to help them along and offer encouragement. I loved that Ryan was involved and he participated for two sessions lasting about 6 months.

At first, he liked it, but this changed over time. His attitude became less enthusiastic each week and he argued with me about going. I was very frustrated because I wanted him enrolled in something with other kids. For whatever reason, he wasn't happy and we didn't enroll for a third session. Was I disappointed? Of course I was, very much so. Should I have forced him to continue for another session? I'll never really know. I'm not inside Ryan's head and don't know why something works or doesn't work for him.

After our attempt at soccer, he laid low for a long time. He was happy to go to school and just come home. I usually had something planned on the weekend such as going to movies, bowling, or visiting our neighborhood bark park so we could play with all the dogs. I felt he wasn't spending enough time engaged with the outside world; it has always been a struggle getting him to do more than just his usual activities alone.

By 8th grade, he became so consumed with only television, computer games, and video games that it was to the exclusion of almost everything else. He used to play on the computer in my office so at least he got out of his room for that. He received a laptop as a gift for his 15th birthday. Now there was no need for him to come out of his room unless it was to use the bathroom or get something to eat. I found this to be most disturbing and my concern that he was becoming more withdrawn had intensified. I knew he needed his down time, and given all that was going on at school, that he wanted to be left alone. I understood this, but to me his alone time was excessive and extreme.

I again looked into the Boy Scout troop near my home. While I didn't believe it was a good fit for Jason, I was told there were now a different group of kids that might be more accepting. Ryan had met a couple of them already because Jason was friends with them. I thought this would be a wonderful opportunity for him. Close to home, he knew a couple of kids and incredible troop leaders.

As usual, Ryan argued about going. I was so upbeat in telling him about the group and really hoped he would change his mind. Our first meeting was really hard. The other kids tried to engage him but he walked around in circles in the corner of the room. He also paced back and forth and only looked down at the floor. I started crying because I had my hopes up that he would enjoy the group. The dads were so sweet and reassured me that everything would be okay. It's not that I was embarrassed; the leaders knew Ryan was on the autism spectrum and had OCD. I was just so sad because I wanted something to work – anything! But this was the first meeting and these things take time.

We went back the following week for another meeting. I made Ryan sit at a table with the two kids he knew and each time he tried to get up, I gave him "the look" and he knew to sit back down. Shortly thereafter, I actually saw him talking to one of the other kids. I was thrilled! I then realized Ryan was talking about one of his favorite shows, Family Guy. This wasn't exactly Boy Scout material but at least he was interacting. I thought he was having a fairly good time but when the meeting was over, he couldn't wait to leave.

The troop was having a campout the following week and they would have loved for Ryan to come. I was so touched that they wanted to include him without even knowing him that well. I told them how much I appreciated their kindness and that in time, I would be ecstatic for Ryan to join them. The next week's meeting came and again, Ryan did not want to go. He's as sweet as he can be, but he sure does have a stubborn streak in him. I told him he was going and there was no discussion.

We went to the meeting but I could see it just wasn't working. Who was I kidding? Maybe this wasn't the right group for him. It's not that I wanted to avoid the aggravation of taking him every week. This didn't bother me in the least. But I could see he just felt out of place. Should I have made him continue in hopes of him eventually feeling more comfortable? Was I letting him win again? It wasn't about winning to me. I just wanted Ryan to find a place in this world that he might enjoy and I could see this wasn't happening here. Yet again, I thanked the dads many times and apologized that I didn't think it would work out. As you would expect, they were more than gracious and of course, the door was always left open.

A few months later, I wanted to try another activity. So in my valiant attempt to once again encourage him to leave his room, I enrolled him in a theatre class for special needs kids. The class has been around for years and was a unique opportunity for kids to participate in a theatre production. They have a recital at the end of each session and the experience of participating in their own role as part of an overall production can be rewarding on many levels. During 7th grade, he was involved in a play at school and had one line. He was so excited to recite those few words and thrilled to have his family come and watch him on stage. Since I thought he enjoyed theatre, I believed the theatre class would be a great match.

When I told him I enrolled him, he was angry that I had done it without checking with him first. I didn't think it would be a problem since he liked his other theatre class; it didn't dawn on me that he would be against the idea. I sure missed the boat on that one. His anger turned into hurt feelings. He was crushed and began crying. I was shocked at his reaction. He proceeded to tell me that he felt betrayed! Betrayed? What had I done to betray him? I was so confused and tried to get my arms around his emotions. He felt I betrayed him because I didn't ask him first. I could see he didn't understand the meaning of the word and explained I didn't betray him.

I emphasized I really thought he would enjoy it and never meant to hurt his feelings. He continued to cry and I promise you they were real tears. I had already paid for the class so there wasn't much I could do. I asked him to please give it a try and that it was possible he just might enjoy it. He didn't believe this was the case and was still angry at me. I finally calmed him down but it took awhile. I really was caught off guard and felt terrible that he was so crushed. He agreed to attend two classes. I explained there were eight classes and attending only two wasn't going to be enough of an indicator whether or not he would like it. Also, paying for the entire session, they were not going to refund my money for the remaining classes.

He dwelled on this for the rest of the evening and the next day when he got home from school. The class was that night and I tried to be enthusiastic in hopes it would rub off on him. No such luck. He then told me on the way to the class, "You thought you knew the cover of my book, didn't you?" It was all I could do to keep from laughing. I knew what he was trying to ask me. He had heard the expression, "Don't judge a book by its cover." Since he enjoyed the theatre class at school, I made the assumption he would enjoy another class outside of school. He didn't want me "judging" him about things like that again and wanted me to know I was mistaken.

Well, it's been four classes so far and he doesn't seem to look forward to it. I know he's counting the classes until it's over. I was really hoping it would click with him and he would want to continue with another class in the fall. I've concluded I have a better chance of losing 15 pounds by summer. I tried something new and it didn't work again. Am I disappointed? I sure am. Is it hard to accept again that another extra-curricular activity didn't work out? Absolutely. But I tell myself again that this is my reality and it is what it is. I can only continue to be on the lookout for future opportunities and hope that the next time, Ryan will embrace the activity.

Summer time – it has its pros and cons. The plusses are that the alarm doesn't go off at 6:00 a.m., there are no homework assignments to be checked, and no early bedtimes to adhere to. Yes, the joys of summer. As a kid, I went to overnight camp when I was six years old. Yes, that was very young but my brothers and sister attended so my mom felt it would be okay. I was very easy; she put me on the plane and I went. I have fond memories so it must have been fine. I then went to day camp for the remainder of the summer and enjoyed this, too. Once I became too old, I became a camp counselor or found a job. I was open to different ideas and I've tried to instill this in my kids.

When they were young, they were okay going to day camp. They attended one camp for a few years and then I found a tennis camp I thought they would like. After doing that for a few years, their needs changed again. As long as they were enrolled in a camp for part of the summer, I was okay with this. I didn't expect them to be programmed the entire time.

When Jason became too old to be a camper he took classes with one of his friends at a local university. Ryan's middle school had a one month summer camp program which was a saving grace. It was through Citizen Schools of Texas and the director was fabulous. She understood special needs kids and always looked out for Ryan. He went from the summer of 5th grade through 7th grade. It was perfect because it ran from 9:00 – 2:30 and was at his school so he already knew the surroundings. It was just enough where he could sleep in a little, be out for part of the day and then come home to have the rest of the day to himself.

Each summer, it was more challenging to find something for Ryan to do than for Jason. Jason usually fell into something to occupy his time but this was not the case for Ryan. This summer, I thought I was going to enroll him in an art camp because I didn't have a lot of choices. While I knew art was not at the top of Ryan's list, he would go swimming every day and this would make up for the art class. I tried to find other camps that would be a better fit but had no luck. Having a child who is not athletic doesn't help. It's also hard when your child is not involved in team sports, but needs something non-competitive and requires the same activities each day. He's more comfortable with that continuity rather than being at a camp where the kids learn a new sport every week.

Fortunately, I received incredible news just two weeks before school year ended and this changed all of our plans. He came home with a notice from the school that our district was offering a social skills program for middle school and high school kids. It was a half day program offered during the month of June at a middle school only twenty minutes away. I immediately called the program coordinator to find out more details and determined it would be wonderful for Ryan. The class has eight kids in it with a special education teacher. The goal is to work on social skills with their peers and to take field trips to apply the social skills learned.

No, it's not Ryan's first choice to attend the program and he'd rather be home all day. I was very positive in telling him about the class and explained he needed to do something for part of the summer. I truly believe this program will help him and that he wants to have friends. I can only hope that he will enjoy being there and pray he even meets a new friend that he can interact with throughout the school year. I'm sure I'll hear complaints when he has to wake up early but that's expected with Ryan. I am elated that our school district is offering this class and that Ryan will be a part of it. It sounds like a fantastic opportunity and is long overdue.

Through the years, I've really tried to expose them to different activities in hopes of sparking their interests. I sometimes lament and wonder if I should have been more forceful and not allowed them to quit. It's that delicate balance of what to do when you want them to continue yet they tell you it's too stressful to juggle everything. I strongly believe you have to encourage your child to try new things because you never know what they'll end up liking. This should be for all children, regardless of having special needs. Jason has evolved these last couple of years so I'm not worried about him. He is more of a self starter and makes plans with his friends and finds activities. For Ryan, I do worry and will for years to come. I will continue my hunt to find an interest for him that does not involve a battery operated controller. Please wish me luck on my search!

Great Strides and Proud Moments!

I am proud of Jason and Ryan in so many ways. What may seem insignificant to most parents is not for me. Parents expect their kids to achieve certain milestones or behave in a certain way and never dream their child will do otherwise. I've never taken anything for granted in life, especially with my kids. Each milestone achieved or venture taken is celebrated. So many things aren't important to me because I'm grateful for the tiniest achievements. We've all heard the phrase, "Everything is relative." This expression has new meaning when applied to my life.

From the early years of sitting up, crawling, walking and being toilet trained, my kids were always delayed. The typical expectations that other parents had when their child should be doing something went out the window very early in my life. I was just happy for progress. Even if it was slow, it was still going in the right direction. I know that being toilet trained is huge for so many parents. While it was important to me, I had so many other problems to cope with that I knew this would happen when they were ready. It took Ryan until he was six years old and I told him there would be no more pull-ups. I knew I picked the right time because he had only one accident since being without them. He still wore pull ups at night but I knew this would end in time. And sure enough, it did.

In our school district, there is a program for elementary school children called the Vanguard Program. Your child has to pass a test and if they're accepted, it's quite an accomplishment. The curriculum is advanced and children are even more prepared for middle school than those children learning the regular education curriculum. All of my friend's kids took the test in hopes of getting in but only a few made it. One of my girlfriends called and was upset because her child didn't get in. She was really disappointed and thought they had a chance. I told her how sorry I was that it didn't work out; it is hard when you want something for your child and it doesn't happen. She then caught herself and said, "I should not be telling you this because look at all you go through." I immediately responded by telling her that I didn't want her to keep her feelings from me because she felt my problems were worse than hers. To my friend, it hurt that her child was not accepted. Hurt is still hurt, regardless of the circumstances or magnitude. I wanted her to know how badly I felt for her and her child. Granted, I understood why she felt she should not have shared her feelings with me. My children could never have applied for this program. But at the time, Jason was mainstreamed for two hours each day and that was two hours more than he had been two years prior. And for that, I was grateful. Like I said, it's all relative.

Safety Patrol – it doesn't seem like a big deal to most parents but it was a huge deal for me. In the latter part of 4th grade, Jason saw how the 5th graders opened car doors for other students, helped students that needed assistance, and monitored the school grounds to make sure everything was okay. He wanted to be a part of that and I was the proudest parent. So many kids with autism don't think outside of themselves and Jason volunteering to help others and commit himself every morning to do this was truly wonderful on his part. The teacher in charge knew Jason and his special needs. She was delighted to have him. We talked about what responsibilities he would have. We made sure he would not be placed in the back of the school where there is little supervision. He needed to be in the front or on the side where there were more adults passing by. Jason was never to be left alone during safety patrol due to his impulsivity and was always to be partnered with a senior patrol leader. He was wonderful during his time with safety patrol. Helping the younger kids and acting as a role model were positive steps for Jason.

When Jason was in 5th grade, he also wanted to enter the school district History Fair. He worked so hard and took great pride in his project. For those who know me, they know that projects are not my strong suit. I used to laugh when I saw some of the other students' projects because there is no way they did them on their own. Clearly, the parents were involved to the point where the project became theirs and not their child's. While it's possible a few of the kids created the projects themselves, it was obvious that most received a lot of help from parents.

It was evident that Jason received very little help from this parent. But his project turned out great and it was a true reflection of what he was capable of. He actually won honorable mention! I was elated beyond words and so excited for him. He was beaming when he told me and we celebrated that night. Proud moments such as these are ones that I truly cherish.

Around the same time, his friends were starting to attend overnight camp. Jason wasn't ready for this and I told him that was fine. Some kids wait and some never go; it's what works best for each kid. I wasn't going to push him even though I went to overnight camp when I was six years old. I trusted that Jason knew if and when he was ready.

We received a flier inviting him to participate at a weekend retreat and he decided to go to that. I was so scared but excited. I talked to the camp director to make sure safeguards were in place to whatever extent was possible. I wanted the camp to be aware of his special needs and handpicked his counselors and cabin mates.

The day I dropped him off, I reminded them again of his autism and impulsiveness. They assured me they would take extra special care. I thanked them profusely for all they were going to do to ensure a wonderful experience for him and I meant every word of it. I knew they had so many kids to manage and that mine was not the only child who had issues. Jason loved the experience and I was so happy he did. He even wanted to enroll for a three week camp session in the summer. I never thought I would hear those words. Was I nervous to send him for three weeks? You bet! Just like any other parent, I am no different. But am I nervous for different reasons than other parents? I sure am because I knew that Jason was not your average kid. Regardless, it was a huge step for him to spend the weekend away and to commit to three weeks away. When the summer came, he was excited to be away for so long. Camp went okay but I don't think it was everything he thought it would be. He attended just the one summer session and that was enough for him. This was fine with me; I wanted for Jason what he wanted for himself.

Both of my sons had their Bar Mitzvahs, a beautiful life cycle event when Jewish boys turn 13 years old. For those of you who don't know, it is when boys are allowed to participate in all aspects of Jewish community life. Prior to their Bar Mitzvah, parents were responsible for their child's adherence to Jewish law. Now, the child is held accountable. During the occasion of their Bar Mitzvah, the child is called to the pulpit to read from the Torah and conduct the service for the congregation. They also interpret the weekly Torah portion and write a speech about what they've learned and how it could apply to their life today. Bar Mitzvahs are one of the many joyous ceremonies in a Jewish boy's life. I wanted to make sure that mine had the honor and pleasure of participating as well.

Jason was absolutely amazing! He conducted the service with his childhood friend and together, they were wonderful. You would have never known that Jason had any special needs. He studied his Torah portion with tenacity until it was perfected. He recited it beautifully along with additional Hebrew prayers and it was flawless. His speech to the clergy and congregation was insightful and thought provoking. While I always knew he was capable of participating in the ceremony, I was concerned about the pressure he would be under in doing so. There was no need for me to be nervous; he shined the entire time. These are the moments in a parent's life that you want frozen in time… When everything is just right and you treasure the moment.

Ryan was a different story because he had difficulty learning Hebrew. Moreover, the concept of religion was too abstract for him and trying to comprehend Torah portions from thousands of years ago was not in his realm of understanding. I knew early on that Ryan's Bar Mitzvah ceremony would differ from Jason's and that of most other kids. While Jason was paired up with one of his friends, I knew this wouldn't work for Ryan. His special needs were more extreme and it was best that he have a service tailored just for him in a way that he could understand. Some of my friends were concerned that I was bothered that his service would be different. But all of this was okay with me, it really was. Nothing could have been further from my mind. I was just happy he was going to participate in his ceremony.

The Rabbi was incredible. He created a service that was ideal and meaningful on Ryan's level. Ryan recited very little Hebrew and spoke mostly in English. It was a shorter service but included the significant prayers with a shortened Torah portion read by the Rabbi. None of this mattered to me. It only mattered that he could shine in his own way and partook in a Jewish tradition so important to our faith. Ryan was absolutely precious! He spoke magnificently and captivated the congregation. I would not have traded this for anything.

Every Jewish child should have a Bar or Bat Mitzvah ceremony that is best suited for their needs. I preach this all the time to other parents of special needs kids. I try to allay their concerns in wondering if it will all work out and how their child will manage during the ceremony. Even if the child only says two words, the fact that they are on the pulpit and being honored is momentous. Our local Jewish community newspaper produces a series of special edition magazines highlighting various traditions. They asked if Ryan could be featured in their Bar Mitzvah issue. I was touched and honored beyond belief. They interviewed me about the steps taken to ensure the ceremony was special for

Ryan and why it was so important to make it happen. The goal for me was to give hope to all parents that anything is possible. I truly hope that I helped other parents.

The following year, when Ryan was in 8th grade, he entered the school Science Fair. His principal wanted all of the students to participate and Ryan was no different. She wanted him to have the experience of creating a project and participating in the Fair. His aide worked with him and they created a project about the properties of magnets. I was relieved the aide was helping him because I knew from my experiences with Jason that I was the weakest link when it came to projects. Parents had to sign a form for their child to participate and Ryan made sure I signed it. He was supposed to return the signed form to his science teacher but the teacher was absent for the next two days.

The Science Fair was the following day and I took Ryan to the school where it was being held. Students were supposed to stand by their projects and wait for their turn to present to the judges. When we arrived, Ryan's project wasn't there. The teacher in charge wasn't sure what happened but thought maybe it was left back at the school. So we drove back to our school in search of his project. She felt terrible; I knew it wasn't her fault. Ryan's teacher was still out sick.

We finally found his project and realized why it didn't make it to the school where the Science Fair was being held. Each project had to have the signed parent authorization form. When his project was brought the previous day, there was no form. The Science Fair leaders would not accept the project unless the form was attached. I asked Ryan about this and why he still had it in his backpack. He said he was supposed to turn it into his teacher but the teacher was out sick. He takes everything so literally and never thought to give it to the substitute teacher. Our school realized what had happened and brought his project over.

When we returned to the school where the fair was being held, I had the form in hand. The judges had already started viewing the various projects and Ryan's project was not on any of their lists. I was crushed because I knew that Ryan planned on "presenting" his project to someone. I approached the program coordinator, who was also a science teacher at this school. I had never met him before and was nervous in approaching him. I knew how busy he was and they had their rules for projects being submitted. He questioned why I was even there because parents were not supposed to attend. I told him about Ryan's autism and with him being in a new environment with a lot of kids, I wanted to stay. He immediately said it was fine. I explained what happened and told him that Ryan wouldn't know that he isn't one of the judges. I asked him to just visit with Ryan, ask questions about his project and allow Ryan the chance to feel he was a part of the judging process. He wasn't supposed to because again, Science Fair had their rules. But he could see how much I wanted this for Ryan. He was so kind. He asked Ryan to explain his project, the steps he took to prove his theory and his conclusions. There was a major disconnect because even though Ryan explained it, the "judge" could not understand. So he asked questions in a different way and Ryan still had difficulty getting the words out. It's not that he was nervous; he was explaining it in "Ryan's way". The judge then drew pictures and asked Ryan to explain what the pictures meant. And Ryan explained it beautifully! I was so proud of him and thanked the teacher so many times for giving Ryan the chance. I had tears in my eyes because he didn't have to "judge" Ryan's project. I was so appreciative and he could see that I was.

When they had the school ceremony later that day, Ryan received his "participation" ribbon. That was enough for me and certainly enough for Ryan. Oddly enough, I was at the grocery store a couple of weeks later and, in the checkout line, the same teacher approached me asking me if I was the parent of the project he judged. When I realized it was him, I was given another opportunity to tell him how grateful I was.

Jason's passion for sports increased dramatically during his teenage years. There was always a sporting event to be watched whether it be professional sports or college games. Jason was there quoting statistics and displaying his enthusiasm for the game. I received an e-mail from the Houston Rockets about a "special" they were offering for a six pack of basketball games. I knew Jason would give anything to attend live basketball games and bought two tickets for each of the six games. I made sure all of the games were on the weekends so they wouldn't interfere with school. He could take a friend which was no problem considering they all loved basketball, too. Most parents would not have done this with a 14 year old but I wanted him to have the joy of attending the games. And he did! He loved it and was so proud to have tickets. I was proud of him too, for being responsible enough to attend these games with his friends and not have a parent beside him.

When he was fifteen years old, he decided to apply for a job being a teacher's assistant at our Sunday school. I encouraged this because he is wonderful with younger children and it was another step in his efforts to take on more responsibility. I was also thrilled that he would be making a little money. Every bit helps with teenagers when their spending habits increase each year. It was helpful that he could finally contribute. He was paired with a wonderful teacher and she loved having Jason as her assistant. He enjoyed helping the other students and again, I was happy he was focusing on others and not himself. So many teenagers are egocentric and Jason is no different. The year of teaching other children was the beginning of his wanting to help others.

In high school, he was inducted into the National Honor Society. It was wonderful to see him rewarded for his hard work. He took pride in this accomplishment and took the role seriously. One of the requirements was to complete volunteer hours and Jason tutored younger students in order to fulfill this obligation. He truly enjoys volunteering and I strongly believe it is a self-esteem booster for him. I always tell him how proud I am of him for wanting to help those in need. He has a huge heart and this parent couldn't be any more proud!

Telling Your Child and Their Teachers

When Jason and Ryan were younger, I didn't think about how or when I would tell them about their autism and OCD. I was too busy making sure they were in the best schools, helping them cultivate friendships, and getting through each day. In my opinion, I don't think there is a set time when you tell your kids about their special needs. Every child is different in what they can grasp and each parent has to gauge when they feel is the right time for their child.

With Jason, it happened when he was in 4th grade. Jason did not enter the public school system until 2nd grade. The students in the schools he attended prior seemed typical to him because this was all he knew. In 2nd grade, he was in a self contained class and then mainstreamed for ancillary classes. In 3rd grade, he was mainstreamed even more but always came back to the self-contained class. Clearly, he knew something was different because the other kids' schedules were nothing like his. I was very close with his teacher and she told me she sensed Jason knew he was different. It was nothing he specifically told her but she felt he realized he was not like the other kids. About the same time, I borrowed a book from a friend that was written by a grandfather to his grandson. It was a wonderful book about the grandfather who wrote letters to his grandson trying to explain to him about his autism and why his grandchild did the things he did.

I took the lead from the grandfather and began explaining to Jason about his autism. I also showed him the book and offered it to him to read as well. I think he read parts of it and it did help him understand why he was the way he was. This was the beginning of my many talks with Jason about autism, ADD, OCD, impulsiveness and anxiety. I tailored each talk to his level and what I felt he could comprehend. It wasn't like explaining diabetes where his blood sugar was tested or creating a diet for him to control the condition. This was much different. It was abstract, unpredictable, and there was no cure.

I've always told Jason my beliefs about the causes of autism. In our early conversations, I explained that his brain was different than other kids' and that he enjoyed talking about things that his friends may not be interested in. I kept my explanations simple and always in a language I felt he understood. I've always believed autism was a genetic disorder and neurologically based. I know there are so many theories as to the cause including the MMR shot, a child's diet, or a lack of the enzyme, secretin, which the body is supposed to produce. These are just a few of the causes out there but I don't believe in any of them. For me, it is about the brains of people with autism; they are just wired differently. I would love to say the cause will be determined in my lifetime but I don't think this is the case. So much research is being done but there is still so much more to be examined.

Jason used to ask me if there was a cure. I told him I didn't believe there was one and that what he had was not something you could take a pill for. Like the many theories as to the cause of autism, there are those who believe there is a cure. I am very happy for those parents who tell me their child has been cured. The child has undergone a medical procedure, had their diet modified, or even grown out of being autistic. Again, I don't believe there is a cure. What I do believe is that once a child receives the diagnosis, all measures possible should be taken so the child receives the help they need. Early intervention is the key, whether that means sending the child to special education schools, to speech therapy, or counseling. It is the parent's responsibility to give their child the help they need to develop compensatory skills for any issues they may have.

Now that Jason is 19 years old, I speak even more openly and frankly. There are many teachable moments because I want him to be aware of what makes him tick and how to navigate his way through life. I don't dwell on it – he is not defined only by his autism. It is only a part of who he is. I never want it being used as a crutch but rather as a reason why he functions the way he does.

Ryan is 16 years old; I have not discussed autism, OCD or anxiety with him. I don't feel the comprehension is there. Ryan is very bright academically in subjects that are concrete. I can't show him autism or OCD on a diagram. I don't think he would understand. He gets very anxious at the end of each school year or when taking standardized tests. He constantly worries that he might fail and not graduate to the next grade. I tell him that the teachers and principal know he always tries his best and they will pass him. I don't think he would grasp the concept that because of his autism label, he takes a modified standardized test and the school would never keep him from graduating.

Ryan has attended public school since kindergarten. He was in self contained classes like Jason but never questioned why. Each school year, he was mainstreamed a little more but with an aide. To this day, he still has not asked me why. He's never asked why he had an aide with him in 6th or 7th grade. It's just the way it was and he accepted it.

During their elementary school years, I believe my kids had the best of both worlds. There is much discussion about self contained classes versus mainstream inclusion. We had the luxury of a self contained class with the benefit of mainstreaming and being with typically developing kids. Is this right for all children? I couldn't even begin to answer this question. No two children with autism are alike. Our state mandates that each child under the autism umbrella has an individualized education plan or IEP in any area the child shows an educational need. The name of these plans varies from state to state. The purpose of the IEP is for parents, teachers, and diagnosticians to create the best program for each child. It is not a cookie cutter process. Quite the contrary, it is an involved method of determining where a child stands academically and socially and the best course of action to promote their growth. It was always a delicate balance because being in the self contained class was emotionally safer for them and the teacher knew how to help them if they were having a difficult day. The mainstream classes offered the opportunity to learn from typically developing kids and opened their eyes to the new ideas these kids had. I didn't have to explain to the mainstream teachers about their needs because the special education teacher took care of this for me. The back and forth communication between them was incredible. If one of the teachers felt the kids needed additional help on a subject, they were sure to let the special education teacher know. If the kids were having a rough day and not up to attending their mainstream class, the mainstream teacher was notified. I was blessed in so many ways that the teachers worked together in the best interest of my children.

When middle school arrived, it was a different story. They were too advanced for a self contained environment and mainstreamed for all classes. While this was nerve-wracking at first, I knew it was the right course for them. It was harder with Jason because he didn't have a teacher's aide like Ryan did in 6th grade. With Jason being more mature, I had to give it a chance and hoped it would work out. Each teacher was supposed to receive my child's folder explaining his diagnosis and the modifications they were supposed to adhere to as agreed upon in the IEP.

I knew how hectic the beginning of the school year was for teachers. I also knew the teachers had a lot of students to keep track of and my children were not the only ones with special needs. I always e-mailed them within the first week or so to introduce myself and to give them an opportunity to ask any questions or express any concerns.

After about a month into the school year, I always arranged for a meeting with them. I wanted to make sure they truly understood autism, OCD, and anxiety and how these disorders manifest themselves in my kids. I also wanted to review the modifications in place regarding preferential class seating, extended time on assignments and taking standardized tests in small groups. All of these accommodations allowed for the optimal learning environment for Jason and Ryan. Meeting with them was also an opportunity to discuss what makes my kids tick and how they think. The teachers needed to know my boys were concrete thinkers and socially immature. So many kids fall through the cracks because our school system is beyond overloaded. There was no way my kids were going to fall through any cracks. The teachers welcomed the advantage of one-on-one time with me so they would know how to interact with my kids. It was critical that they know if there is a thunderstorm, Ryan shuts down and will not be able to focus in class. Equally important, they needed to know that my kids were THE rule police. If you tell them something, they will listen and not question you. If the assignment schedule changes, you must tell them more than once. You could not assume that they understood this "change" the first time it was explained to them. All of these things and more were discussed in my initial meeting.

Throughout the year, there were many e-mails, phone calls, and follow up meetings – all for the benefit of Jason and Ryan. It was a collaborative effort and one that certainly paid off.

It Takes a Village

Most of us have heard this expression before and would agree that it does take a village to raise a child. I needed multiple villages to help me help my children progress through life. There have been so many doctors, schools and teachers. Add to them, all of the extracurricular activities and organizations that accepted my kids without question. All of these "villages" were important at various times in my life. While at the end of the day, making sure that Jason and Ryan were taken care of was the responsibility of their dad and me, we could not do it ourselves and the professionals along the way that helped us were instrumental in each child's success.

When I look back at the number of speech therapists, occupational therapists, case managers and in-home trainers that have been in my home, it is astonishing. Each of them made my life a little bit easier and they cared enough to want to help my kids. I fondly remember two of the home trainers who made a huge impact on both kids. These women will always have a special place in my heart. The creativity they used to engage Jason and Ryan and their never ending kindness toward our family is something I will never forget.

There have been so many private and public schools, and so many teachers. The concerted effort taken by them through the years was an integral part of this village. Teachers can have a profound effect on any child and with mine, the effect was even greater. Jason and Ryan were so easily influenced and we were fortunate to have teachers that were positive role models. Both kids have always had tremendous respect for their teachers and looked to them for support and guidance.

Fortunately, they looked to the right place. We all know that teachers don't go into the profession to strike it rich and retire early. They teach because they want to impact a child's life. While I admit there were a few teachers that were not the greatest in working with my kids, they tried to the best of their ability. The elementary school teachers in their self-contained classes were extraordinary. They went above and beyond and I doubt that Jason and Ryan will ever truly be able to appreciate how much they did for them.

The mainstream teachers from elementary school through high school have also been my heroes. The countless e-mails, phone calls and teacher conferences were always met with kindness and a genuine desire to do whatever it takes to help Jason and Ryan succeed. They were not special education teachers and did not have formal training on what it takes to work with kids like mine, but they rose to the occasion time and time again and I applaud them for their sincere efforts.

I love to bake and would always bring something sweet to the meetings or just drop desserts off at the teachers' lounge. It was my way of telling them how much I appreciated them and that I never took them for granted. Some parents would buy expensive presents for the teachers at holiday time or the end of the year. I wasn't able to do that and hope that my endless compliments and desserts let them know how grateful I was and will always be.

The teachers handled the day-to-day rituals of teaching, but the principal and administrative staff were equally important. The positive attitude of any school and its teachers begins at the top. There is one principal who truly stands out, Jason's assistant principal in middle school. I promise you she is one of the main reasons we survived. She worked with me to educate his teachers each year to make sure they understood Jason and his needs. If he was having a rough day, he could always go to her office to calm himself down. Her assistant was an absolute gem. Jason could always come to her if the principal was unavailable and she would drop everything to help him.

As Jason moved on to high school, the assistant principal at his middle school was promoted to being a principal at her own middle school. Since I was looking for a middle school for Ryan, she made sure to sign the transfer form so he could attend. We were not zoned to her school but this didn't matter. Her assistant moved with her and together, they both looked out for Ryan during his middle school years. They had a wonderful aide for Ryan in the 6th grade; this was astounding considering the tight school budgets. I never dreamed any public school would provide this for Ryan but his principal made it happen.

Ryan's aide was so kind and having him that year and part of the year in 7th grade was such a blessing. I could call him on his cell phone or e-mail him with any questions. He truly cared about Ryan and wanted him to excel. I realize that in my earlier chapters, I expressed frustration and disappointment with Ryan's 8th grade year. It was a terrible year but it wasn't for lack of trying on the school's part. There were a number of difficult kids and the school tried to manage them as best they could. Bullies should not be tolerated; it happens everywhere and while it wasn't right, the teachers tried their best.

Another village important to my family was my Temple. When the kids were younger, we often attended Friday night services with other families. It was wonderful to attend the monthly family service with our friends and enjoy dinner afterwards. The clergy always welcomed Jason and Ryan. Most of the time, everything went well. But there was an incident I'll never forget. Unfortunately, it was one of the most trying experiences I had ever had. Jason was 9 years old and Ryan was almost 6. The Rabbi called all the kids up to the pulpit to help him during the service. While the kids were up there, the Rabbi addressed the congregation, but Jason and Ryan misinterpreted what he was saying. They acted out due to their confusion.

The Rabbi didn't do anything wrong; neither did Jason or Ryan. They just didn't understand. He had to stop the service three times. It got so out of hand that the Cantor, one of the other clergymen also leading the service, picked up Ryan to calm him. I wanted to crawl under a rock. What were the other parents thinking? If I went to get both kids from the pulpit, it could have created even more of a disruption. The Rabbi was trying to conduct his service and I didn't want to interfere. Yet, I felt awful that this was happening. Tears began to well up in my eyes. It was all I could do to make it through the rest of the service.

Finally, the Rabbi instructed all of the kids to return to their seats. I wasn't angry at my kids. Not at all; they were having a rough time. Believe me, my kids can be brats just like other kids. But this was not one of those times. The most significant part of this story is that when we were leaving the sanctuary, I told our Cantor, "I am SO sorry." It was obvious I was upset and felt terrible for what had happened. He immediately said it was okay and not to worry. He said, "We want you to be here and we want your children to be here. Don't ever feel you can't bring them. We will work this out."

I cannot tell you how relieved I was to hear those words and I thanked him with all my heart. I cried driving home and then called the Rabbi to apologize. As always, he was so compassionate and reassuring. He told me that no apology was needed. He, too, stressed that he wanted all of us to attend services and be a part of the congregation. He emphasized that we would continue to work this out as each new situation arose. His words were of enormous comfort to me.

The next day, I called a dear friend of mine who also has a child with autism. We frequently call each other and the conversation often begins with, "I have a story that only you can understand...." As always, she understood and knew only too well.

Fast forward a few years. Ryan is now 10 years old. We were attending a service again, but it was just the two of us this time. While this was not a family service geared toward young children, I felt he was able to sit through the service with me as the sanctuary was most familiar to him.

For whatever reason, he was more sensitive that night and more fidgety. He kept moving around and bouncing back and forth in his chair. I don't know why and while I tried to gently calm him down, my efforts failed. There were two elderly women sitting behind us and I could tell they were annoyed. I felt terrible and I apologized because I knew his restlessness was disrupting the service for them. I thought it would be okay if we continued to stay. Halfway through the service, one of the women said to me in a condescending voice, "There are babysitters for babies like him!" I froze – I was completely paralyzed.

I'm not usually that way and typically speak up to defend myself and my child. But my defenses were really low that day and I wasn't myself. It took me a few minutes to get over the shock of what she said. I couldn't take it anymore; I looked at the woman and said, "I'm sorry if my son bothered you. He has special needs and is doing the best he can." The lady just looked at me. I took Ryan's hand and we left. Other congregants saw what happened and tried to get me to stay. But I just couldn't. At that moment, I just couldn't deal with it.

Ryan asked me why we were leaving before the service ended. I told him I wasn't feeling well and needed to go home. Within the hour, I received no less than four phone calls – including one from the Rabbi. One of the congregants had told him what happened and he wanted to make sure I was okay. He said that we are always welcome and he wanted us to continue to attend services. The other congregants called to tell me they went up to the lady who made the remark and let her have it. I'm sure they did. While I was touched by their support and caring for my welfare, I was not surprised by this woman's remarks to me. People are ignorant and make judgments all the time. If I remembered who she was now, I would gladly drop off a copy of this book. She could definitely benefit from it.

That experience was one of the worst I had ever encountered and I'm happy to say we were never treated like this again by a fellow congregant. While it was an isolated incident, it's been six years since it happened and I still remember it as clear as day.

I mentioned earlier how understanding the Rabbis were during their Bar Mitzvahs. Long before then and from the very beginning, the religious school director made sure that my kids' needs were met at Sunday school. They worked with me to choose just the right teacher for each child every year. I loved every teacher and they treated my kids like gold. They were warm, understanding and nurturing.

Jason was easier to place in class because he was higher functioning while Ryan was a bit more challenging due to his delays being more pronounced. If aides were needed, the Temple provided them. They could not have been more accommodating; I could not have been more grateful. While Jason attended the regular Sunday School all the way through his Bar Mitzvah, this was not the case with Ryan. By the time he reached 5th grade, the gap between him and the other kids had widened so much that I didn't feel it was in his best interest to stay in that class. The Temple did not ask me to withdraw from their program; I just knew in my heart that it wasn't working any longer.

I've said it before and I'll say it again; all parents have to be realistic about what's best for their children. I know parents who are not realistic and this is so unfair to the child, teachers, and other students in the class. The teachers in our Sunday School are not special education teachers.

Each year, I consulted with the religious school director to make sure the teachers felt comfortable having my kids in their classes. This open dialogue is what allowed me as a parent to make the best decisions possible. When it came time to withdraw Ryan, they would have kept him in their program because he was so sweet and easy to work with. But there was more to it than that. I wanted him to have the opportunity to learn as much about Judaism as possible. Special education teachers and a smaller class setting would be the best option to afford him this chance. The Jewish community, through the Jewish Federation of Houston, had a class called "Kesher". Kesher is the Hebrew word for "link." One of the main goals in creating this class was to link children like mine to the Jewish community and our Jewish heritage. I contacted the program coordinator; she welcomed Ryan with open arms. It was difficult to make this change but this wasn't about me; it was about Ryan. He always came first and always will.

The Kesher teachers were fabulous! The class size was small and the curriculum was geared to a level that worked best for kids like Ryan. Religion can be a very abstract concept for kids on the autism spectrum. It's hard to explain to them what happened thousands of years ago and why we practice the rituals we do today. Do I think that Ryan grasped the concepts taught? I'm not sure. He basically repeated what he had been taught and it's hard to gauge how much he truly comprehended. But that's okay with me. The important part of all of this is that the Jewish Federation, in conjunction with the Temples, offered this class and works hard to make sure that all kids with special needs can be exposed to Judaism.

Jason continued attending his weekly religious education class through the 8th grade and Ryan stopped attending weekly classes once he had his Bar Mitzvah. Jason could have continued through the 12th grade but with the pressures of high school, he elected not to. Ryan had his share of stress with middle school and this is why I felt it was too much for him to continue attending classes. I know the door is always open for Ryan to attend Sunday School should his circumstances change. I strongly believe religious education is very important and that it lays the foundation for practicing in your adult years. I attended religious school classes until I graduated high school. For my kids, it didn't work out this way. To this day, I often lament that this has happened and wonder if I should have pushed them more. It is one of the many decisions made that I will always wonder about.

Fortunately, Jason became involved in a Jewish youth group in high school where he could bond with other Jewish kids, participate in Jewish programs, and connect with the community. The adviser of his chapter was incredible! She knew of Jason's needs and encouraged his involvement each year. She watched him grow through the years and was so proud of him. I also thanked her many times for watching over Jason and her dedication to the chapter.

Another wonderful organization and "village" that has helped my family through the years is "The Friendship Circle". It was founded in Detroit in 1994 with just 8 families. Since 1991, Friendship Circles have been started in over 80 locations in 22 states and 7 Countries. I'm proud to write that Houston is home to one of them. The tireless efforts of the Rabbi and his wife, his assistant, and volunteers are to be celebrated. Their mission is to lend a helping hand to families who have children with special needs and involve them in a range of social and Judaic activities. They match teenage volunteers with kids like Ryan to come into our home for weekly visits and just be a friend. We were one of the first families to participate and the volunteers are amazing. When Ryan first began having his "friends" visit, he was distant at times. With each year, he has become more responsive. This past year has been the best. Two boys come each week to play video games or just watch television. I tell the boys and their parents all the time how much their visits mean to Ryan and our family. It's so important to me that they know how thankful I am.

Teenagers today lead very hectic lives and their commitment to visit Ryan is commendable. Their parents deserve equal praise because they are the ones responsible for dropping them off and picking them up. This is no easy task because they, too, are juggling work and other responsibilities. All of the volunteers will always be special to me because they cared. They could have easily declined participating in The Friendship Circle and given the reason that they were too busy. I thank G-d every day that they didn't.

I have two new villages that have been recently added to my world. The first is Trinity University in San Antonio where Jason will be attending college. As I write these words, I am beaming with pride at his accomplishments and acceptance to this prestigious university. It is a small school with only 2,600 students and I am thrilled he will be attending in the fall. From our initial contact with their admissions department, I knew this would be an exceptional home for Jason these next four years. I've already had numerous conversations with their financial aid office, special services department, and health services. Each person I spoke with was so kind and more understanding than I ever imagined possible.

When sending their kids to college, many parents can attend the parent orientation, say their good-byes and then return home. Not me. I've had numerous conversations with the Director of Special Services and an assistant at the Department of Health Services. I couldn't just send Jason to Trinity without safeguards in place to make sure they were aware of his special needs. I've made sure I know what help Jason can take advantage of if needed and even the hours of the student clinic. The admissions department was cognizant of his needs because his essay was entitled "My Life with Autism and ADHD". But I could not assume that this information would be conveyed to the other departments within the university.

Please don't think that I want Jason to be labeled - quite the contrary. I want his professors and peers to see him for the amazing young man that he is. He should not be defined by his issues but supported in his efforts to cope with them. I just want to make sure that I've done my due diligence prior to him attending. This includes establishing relationships with these departments to ensure a smooth transition his freshman year and beyond. Jason's autism and other problems are not going to evaporate when he goes to college. I'd be fooling myself if I thought that I didn't have to have these safeguards in place. Having a child and even adult with special needs always means having to be a step ahead to afford them every opportunity to be successful. Am I a bit apprehensive? Of course I am. But being a small school, knowing that I'm only 3 ½ hours away and establishing my contacts now in case Jason has any problems so that I don't have to react to something in crisis mode - all of these factors allay my concerns to some degree.

I want these next four years to be another positive layer in his foundation of lifelong learning. While there might be a few cracks in the layer, I know Jason will have the support he needs to repair them and begin building the next layer.

The second village recently added to my world is Ryan's new school he's starting in the fall, Bellaire High School. You have no idea how much I wish I could write that I feel great about this decision. Nothing would make me happier than believing it's the best school for him. Sadly, I am terrified. It has nothing to do with the staff I've met thus far. It's just the opposite.

The Special Ed Coordinator has been wonderful in working with me to meet Ryan's needs and planning out his class schedule. I've toured the school and discussed Ryan with the assistant principal; he could not have been more understanding and caring. Ryan has toured the school and while it was foreign to him, he seemed okay. Naturally, he was confused because he isn't familiar with the surroundings. This will take time. So what is the problem?

The school is huge with 3500 kids attending. I lose sleep that Ryan will get lost in the crowd. The school is a multistory building with three levels. Ryan will have classes on all three floors. This is the high school I am zoned to and while they have a good reputation and a fantastic principal, I'm not convinced it is the best match for Ryan. I know that no school is perfect, but I'm not looking for perfection. One of my philosophies in life is that I go by the 80/20 theory. If 80% of the time something is going well, I'm pretty content. There will always be that 20% where there are kinks to be worked out or maybe something isn't what I expected it to be. I can accept this and work out those issues that arise. But with such a large high school and huge class sizes, I agonize as to whether or not I am making the right decision. So far, I've put the following safeguards in place or will reach out to the following organizations/faculty members when they return from the summer break:

1. A study hall period is scheduled for every day. He'll be able to get help with assignments or if he just needs down time, he'll have a place to go. The trouble is that Ryan is not the best at asking for help. It's hard to say if it's because he gets intimidated or just doesn't know how to ask for it. I've explained so many times that the teachers are there to answer questions and guide him. It just doesn't sink in like I'd hoped it would. I'm sure I'll be contacting the teacher to make sure Ryan is taking advantage of the opportunity to receive extra help.

2. Rather than enrolling him in PE, he's enrolled in ROTC. I believe this is a better choice because the class is very rule oriented and structured. Ryan did not take PE in middle school because kids have to dress out in a locker room and this could get complicated for him. He believes that when you get dressed for something, it's done in a closed room with no one else around. Being around all of the other kids in a locker room would not work and he could be the target of inappropriate behavior. With ROTC, students wear a uniform to school once a week which eliminates the locker room problem. In addition, Ryan is not athletic or coordinated at all and I know how competitive and judgmental kids can be. He could easily be made fun of because of his lack of athletic skill.

3. He likes to play chess. I'll e-mail the teacher in charge to let them know that Ryan will be joining the club. They meet during lunch, which will hopefully offer him some companionship so he's not alone.

4. The school also has a "Best Buddies" program that is like the Friendship Circle. They match up typically developing high school kids with special needs kids so they have a friend at school and can participate in activities together. I'll make sure he is added to their list so a student can be paired up with him.

5. He'll attend "Cardinal Camp" – a 12-hour orientation program for incoming freshman being held 2 weeks prior to school starting. It's not as though I can just drop him off at the front door of the school. I'll walk him in, stay a little bit to hear what they have to say, and make sure he feels comfortable. I'll contact the teacher in charge so they, too, are aware of Ryan's special needs.

6. Each student is assigned a counselor. I've already e-mailed Ryan's, but she is expecting a baby right about the time school begins. She plans on returning to work in October and felt badly she wouldn't be there when school begins. I'll contact her department head to see who I can meet with in case we need another resource during her absence.

7. I'll be e-mailing the teachers once his schedule is confirmed. I want to give them a heads up and answer any questions they may have. I know how overloaded they are and it's very hard to keep track of each student.

The list above may seem long to you or extreme in nature. I promise you it isn't. It's what parents like me must do so their child has the best chance for success. I realize that

Ryan is not the first special needs student the high school has worked with and he will not be the last. Previous students like him have managed just fine. I tell myself this over and over but it doesn't help. Oh, how I wish it did! When I went to pick up the summer reading schedule, summer school was in session. The other students looked so old and so tall. By the time I got back to my car, my eyes were filled with tears. High school is a major adjustment for any child. For Ryan, it is 20 times more.

You might wonder "Why am I sending him to a school I'm not comfortable with"? At this point in time, it's the best public school choice for me. I wish I could have sent Ryan to the public high school Jason attended. Unfortunately for Ryan, that school has a policy where students are required to take college classes beginning in the 10th grade. While Ryan is bright, his middle school principal didn't feel this would work well for him and it would be too much pressure.

There is a very small private school that I would give anything to send Ryan to. I know he would receive an enormous amount of attention because the class sizes are so small. Unfortunately, the school is very costly and they don't have a scholarship program. So for now, he's in the public high school in our neighborhood and I will continue to do everything possible to make it work for him. I put on a very brave front when Ryan is around and will continue to introduce him to as many teachers and support staff as possible. I will say many prayers and I'm sure I'll be baking a lot this year to let them know how much I appreciate their help and guidance.

My own personal village is my family and friends. Since the beginning, they have been an invaluable source of support. Their love and caring is priceless! As I became knowledgeable about Jason and Ryan's special needs, I educated them as well. Once the social skills that needed to be learned were mastered, there were new skills to be tackled. The obsessions or anxieties of the day that needed to be coped with were sometimes managed or replaced by new ones. It is a lifelong learning process for all of us because their needs are ever changing.

All of the villages I've mentioned have touched my life in ways I never could have imagined. Because it takes so many people to raise kids like mine, I'm sure there will be more villages added on every year. I will seek out help from each of them. I will educate each of them about special needs. And I will be saying thank you to each of them so many times because I will never take them for granted and always make sure they know how grateful I am.

If I Only Had a Crystal Ball

I know people who thrive on the element of surprise. They appear to relish in the fact that life can be so unpredictable. I wish I was one of those people because if I was, my life would be a lot easier. I wouldn't take everything to heart so much and wonder why things happen the way they do. Intellectually, I know it doesn't help to ask, "Why?" But in my heart, I often search for answers. Why do my kids have to struggle with autism, OCD, anxiety and ADHD? Kids have enough to cope with growing up, why add more? They're just kids.

As a parent, watching them struggle through the years has been excruciating. Nothing in life comes easily to them and it breaks my heart. I am a strong believer that everything happens for a reason, even though we do not know why. But this belief has been tested so many times. I remember years ago reading "Why Bad Things Happen to Good People". It is a beautifully written book written by Rabbi Kushner after he lost his son to a premature aging disease. The book addresses the questions we may have about human suffering. I've also counseled with my own Rabbi as I've struggled with why G-d would allow certain things in my life to happen. People always used to say to me "G-d only gives you what you can handle." At times, I would become angry because I felt as though my plate was overflowing and there was too much to cope with in my life. Having people tell me that I should be able to manage what I had been dealt with because G-d knew what I could handle – this was of little comfort to me.

So I asked my Rabbi if he thought that G-d only gives us what we can handle. I was stunned to hear his answer. He said "No. I think that sometimes G-d does give us too much to handle. We then have to look inside ourselves to find that inner strength to help us cope during these difficult times. We all want freedom of choice but with that freedom, all of us can make poor choices. As a result, those choices can make our life more painful." Those words were spoken to me in 1998. I found a sense of peace in them then and continue to even today. They helped me to not be angry at G-d and it was as if a weight had been lifted. In helping friends or family cope with their struggles, I've repeated those same words.

Many times, I've had people tell me, "You are so lucky. I've seen kids so much worse off than yours. Your kids are going to be just fine." I thought to myself – really? I guess they must have that crystal ball to know what the future holds and how everything will turn out. I could not imagine telling anyone that about anything. None of us knows what tomorrow will bring. It's not that I'm angered by their words. I realize that people sometimes say something because they don't know what else to say or they are trying to comfort me. Unfortunately, their words do not help. All I ever ask for is their understanding and patience if my kids are having a rough day.

If I knew years ago how my life would have turned out today, I imagine I would have done some things differently. That crystal ball sure would have come in handy. I know that in raising Jason and Ryan, I've done the best I can. I love them with all my heart and always try to set the best example. But I often lament and wonder if I've made the right decisions or wish I had been more firm at times. Did I choose the right school? Should I have made them pursue some hobby or sport? If only I had pushed for them to try more of a variety of foods, maybe they wouldn't be so limited today. If only I had pushed more to do other activities together as a family.

Ryan and I still go to the movies together and out to his favorite restaurants. He'll sometimes watch his television shows with me and I love that he wants to be with me. The three of us used to do these things together and I was so happy when we did. I realize it isn't unusual that kids want to break away from their parents; I know I did the same thing when I was a teenager. I just wish it were different right now.

With Jason wanting to be more with his friends or have his own down time and with Ryan being more withdrawn, those times together are very few. I look at other families and how they frequently spend time together. It makes me sad that the three of us aren't like this. Maybe it will change again in the years to come and I can only hope.

With Jason going off to college, I have wonderful visions of Ryan and me going to visit him for the night – meeting his new friends and spending time together in San Antonio. I will do everything I can to make this happen.

I know my sons have made tremendous strides in their development and I believe that part of this is because of them having me as their loving mother. I'm not trying to sing my own praises, but truly believe that showing affection to your children and telling them how proud you are will comfort them during difficult times. I always make sure that my last words to my kids when they walk out the front door are, "I love you." It doesn't solve their problems or prevent them from having a bad day. I just want them to always remember that they are loved and to give them some reassurance. Having them hear those words from me time and time again - I never want them to forget.

Do I still wish I had that crystal ball or could turn back the clock today? Absolutely, I think about it often. At times, it is very difficult for me to accept that my life has turned out the way that it has and I have to live with some of the decisions I've made. Acceptance has always been hard for me and as much as I tell myself and my friends that we all have to accept what is, this doesn't make it easier for any of us. I wish that part of my personality would change but it hasn't yet. At 48 years old, I don't know that it will. We can all change to some degree but at the end of the day, we are who we are. In my efforts to be the best person I can each day, I know that I always have the best of intentions. I can only continue to teach this to Jason and Ryan and work with them to accept their lives as they are and to be the best person they can be.

Final Thoughts

When I began writing this book, I wasn't sure how many chapters it would be or how long it would take me. I've had so many stories and thoughts through the years and a vision of how I wanted to share them with you. When it came time to formulate them into a book, it was at times a daunting task. Yes, it was cathartic in many ways but I was sometimes discouraged because I couldn't seem to get the words out in the way that I wanted and would rewrite some chapters numerous times. How did I finally finish? My desire to help others in my shoes superseded any frustrations I encountered. I also had the love and support of my family and friends who reminded me that writing a book would do so much to educate the world about special needs.

People often ask me how I manage and tell me I deserve an award. I am no different than anyone else and certainly have not earned any awards. We all do what it takes to make it through the day because we don't have a choice. Life is not a dress rehearsal and every moment should be cherished. Each person who cares should be valued. I've tried to stress this to Jason and Ryan. They have a loving father and step-family, devoted grandparents, an extended family, and friends who care so much about them. Not everyone is as fortunate. I have a wonderful mother who has inspired me my entire life. She has been through so much but continues to smile through it all. Thinking of her and what she has had to survive has helped me to cope with my own problems.

When I became a single parent, a number of people told me they wondered if I could ever find a man who would accept me and my kids. I explained that while I didn't want to go through the rest of my life alone, I prayed that at some point in my life, I would meet a wonderful man who cared about me and my kids as well. We come as a package and this package cannot be divided. Yes, there were many lonely times and I often wondered if my days would turn brighter. That day happened in January of 2006. I met Craig and we've been dating for 5 years. He has learned so much about autism, OCD and anxiety and he, too, educates others when given the chance. He is the love of my life, and his mother and daughter have become my family.

We often get asked when we'll marry. This is not on our agenda and being in a committed relationship works beautifully for us. When the kids are grown, I would love to. But for now, my life is so complicated and I'm concerned about the stress it would put on me and the kids if we blended families. I know plenty of people who do; it's just not for me and was never something I considered.

Craig shares my passion in wanting to raise awareness about my kids' disabilities. We've created a 501(c)(3) foundation, Ryan's World, to raise money and augment the efforts of organizations in Houston dedicated to helping families with special needs. There are several incredible groups that organize programming and support services, and we want to help them in their cause. Being a new foundation, it takes time to build resources but Craig and I are dedicated to helping our community and giving back as much as we can. Like many cities, Houston has been strained by the economy and there is a desperate need for more dollars. These groups have done so much for my family. I will be elated when I can help them in return.

Another passion I have is traveling the country to speak to people everywhere about the special needs world. I've spoken to students and community groups in Houston and welcome the opportunity to share my message with anyone and everyone. I want to continue to reach out and educate others. The groups I've spoken to thus far have all told me that they learned so much and I allowed them to see what life is like for people different than themselves. Some of the audience members I spoke to were not aware of the challenges for kids like mine.

If my life mirrored the life of someone I was speaking before, I was told they found comfort in listening to a kindred spirit. I cannot begin to tell you much it means to me to help others and make an impact on someone's life. So many people have helped me and changed my life. The fact that I am able to give back is ever-so-important to me.

As I said in my first chapter, I don't want your pity and I can promise you my children don't either. Jason and Ryan are incredible kids who make a difference in this world and will continue to in the years to come. Yes, they have many challenges they've had to cope with and there are more to come; life has not been fair to them in many ways. Instead of feeling sorry for them and defining them only by a label, give them a chance. Instead of seeing them as people with special needs, try to see them as people who are just special. See them for the kind souls that they are and your life will be enriched for knowing them.

I want to thank you for joining me in my world. There are many books you could have chosen to read and I am honored that you chose mine. I hope you have learned something from the stories I've shared. There will be more to share in the coming years but, for now, what I have written will have to do as every story has to have an end. In the beginning, I wrote that I wanted to open your eyes; open your mind; and, most of all, open your heart. The next time you see someone acting in an unusual way, I hope you judge them less quickly or not at all. I hope that you remember how you felt when you read about my experiences. I hope you could understand that there was much more to my story than you could possibly know. I hope you begin to look at others in a different light and maybe when you are with family and friends, you will try to help them see that everything they assume is not always what it appears to be. If you can influence others, as I try to, then my mission to raise awareness and compassion will be accomplished.

Please continue the journey at **www.judysworld.info**! Book her as a speaker for your city, order more books or read her blog. Always wanting to connect with her readers, tell her more about you by registering on her website. You'll be in the know about her travels and she would love to meet you when she's in your city! If you think there is a group that is interested in her message, let her know and she'll reach out to them!